YOUR MONEY MATTERS

Rules Nobody Taught You

Verses Kindler Publication

Verses Kindler Publication.

Website: www.verseskindlerpublication.com

YOUR MONEY MATTERS- Rules nobody taught you

By: Mr. Shankar T

ISBN: 978-93-47494-35-2

1st Edition

Price: INR 499/$22

Disclaimer

YOUR MONEY MATTERS- Rules nobody taught you is authored by Shankar T. The entirety of this published work comprises the original content of the author, who has undertaken diligent efforts in its editing. The characters depicted herein may be fictitious or inspired by real events; however, they are not intended to cause offense or represent any prejudice against any caste or system. Any similarity to the names of actual individuals, locations, or institutions is purely coincidental and serves the narrative. The author bears sole responsibility for the originality of this work; the publisher assumes no liability thereof.

Table of Content

Chapter 1: The Cost of Not Knowing - Why Financial Literacy Matters

Rahul's Wake-Up Call

Rahul, a 21-year-old engineering student, thought money was something only "grown-ups" needed to worry about. His pocket money and scholarships covered food, gadgets, and endless café outings. He assumed that once he got a job, the paycheques would solve everything.

But when he graduated, it reality hit. Rent, utility bills, and loan repayments piled up. His salary looked big on paper, but disappeared in the first two weeks. He had never budgeted, never saved, and never thought about insurance. By month three, Rahul was borrowing from friends just to survive. He realised too late that ignoring money only made life harder.

The Price Tag You Never Saw Coming

It's strange how we're taught to solve trigonometric equations, write chemical formulas, and even memorize the life cycle of a frog, but not how to handle the first ₹10,000 we earn.

By the time most Indian youngsters finish their education, they know how to write a five-paragraph essay on GDP but don't understand how to manage their own. Some don't even know what GDP means. And yet, every day, they're making money decisions, consciously or not.

Do I spend ₹2500 on that limited-edition sneaker?

Should I apply for a credit card that offers "free" lounge access?

Can I afford to split rent with my friends on a flat that "looks like Goa inside"?

Is that "guaranteed" double-return stock tip from a Telegram group real?

No textbook has prepared them for these. No curriculum has ever said: "This is how money can either ruin you or raise you."

The truth is simple and terrifying: you either learn about money early, or pay the price for not knowing.

Real Stories, Real Stakes

Let me start with two short, painful stories, both real, both familiar.

A teenager, desperate to look cool in his college group, begged his parents for a sports bike worth ₹1.7 lakh. His father, a clerk, and his mother, a homemaker, hesitated but gave in, taking a personal loan with EMIs that ate up 40% of their monthly income. All so their son wouldn't feel "less than" his richer peers.

The costs did not stop even there. With a bike comes its maintenance - petrol, servicing, and sometimes, even some repair work. So, his parents kept paying.

Another young man, deeply empathetic to his family's financial condition, decided he didn't want to wait for years to become their “provider.” So he turned to what many others are turning to: cricket betting apps. The promise was irresistible: turn ₹10 into ₹1000 overnight. He lost ₹80,000 before his parents found out and cleared his debts.

The saddest part? Neither of them knew any better. And that’s exactly the problem.

Why We Don’t Talk About Money

Let’s face it: In most Indian homes, money is a closed topic. A room you're not allowed to enter.

As children, we’re told, “Don’t worry about money, just study.”

As teens, we hear, “You’ll understand when you start earning.”

And when we finally earn? We’re told, “Now you should already know.”

Where in this timeline was the space to ask questions? Who taught us how to read a payslip? When did we learn the difference between “spending smart” and “spending rich”?

The cultural discomfort around financial conversation is part of the problem. In many Indian families, especially middle-class ones, money is either a source of fear or pride, but rarely education. Parents either overprotect their children financially or expect them to “figure it out” when they grow up.

We hand over debit cards before handing over budgeting basics. We give UPI access before explaining compounding interest. We tell them "Don't waste" without ever defining what that even means.

Why Financial Literacy Isn't Just About Numbers

Here's a bold statement: Financial literacy is more important than academic performance. It's not just about how much you earn. It's about how you live with what you have.

Financial literacy means knowing:

- What you can afford vs. what you want.
- How loans work, and why not all credit is bad.
- How saving early adds up faster than earning late.
- Why investing ₹1000 at 18 is smarter than investing ₹10,000 at 30.
- How the tiniest money habit today builds your financial identity tomorrow.

It's a life skill, not a math problem.

And like all skills, it should be learned, not assumed, and definitely not postponed.

Most people think financial knowledge is only for the "finance guys." The ones who work in banks or handle stock markets. The truth is, money affects everyone. You can be a filmmaker, coder, designer, writer, singer, gym trainer, doctor, teacher, or still figuring life out, and you will have to manage money.

If you don't know how, someone else will manage it for you. And not always in your best interest.

When Not Knowing Becomes a Debt

Money, by itself, is neutral. It doesn't have emotions. It doesn't care whether you're wise or reckless. It simply reacts to how you use it. And the harsh reality is: money punishes ignorance faster than anything else in life.

A simple oversight, like not knowing the difference between your account balance and your credit limit, can spiral into months of EMIs. Not knowing what "interest-free" really means can cost you 18% per annum. Skipping the fine print can drag your savings into late fees, penalties, and collection calls.

Most young people don't make poor decisions because they're careless. They make poor decisions because they were never shown what "careful" looks like.

That's the scariest part: you can fall into financial trouble without doing anything "wrong" by your standards.

And it usually starts small:

- A pizza every weekend, when your monthly budget barely covers your metro pass.
- An iPhone EMI you can't track because the job you planned to get didn't come through.
- A college trip booked on someone else's suggestion, charged to a card you didn't understand.

One missed payment turns into a cycle. One poor choice becomes a pattern. And slowly, your entire identity starts to feel burdened by the weight of money you don't control.

Guilt and Silence: A Cost No One Calculates

Imagine this: You've maxed out your credit card buying stuff you didn't need. You're 21. You've been avoiding the statements. You haven't told your parents because "they'll freak out." You've stopped hanging out with friends because you feel ashamed. You scroll past all the finance content online because it makes you feel stupid.

This is the real cost of financial illiteracy. Not just the money, but:

- The isolation.
- The anxiety.
- The hit to your self-confidence.
- The loss of control over your own story.

It's like carrying a backpack filled with bricks, invisible to the world, but heavy on every step you take.

One of the biggest lessons you'll ever learn about money is this: Avoidance is always more expensive than awareness.

The "Live for Today" Trap

Now, let's talk about one of the most dangerous mindsets circulating in today's youth culture: YOLO. You Only Live Once.

Sounds exciting, right? And sure, life is meant to be lived. No argument there.

But here's the catch: "live for today" has somehow mutated into "spend for today." It's become less about enjoying the present and more about ignoring the future.

Social media doesn't help. You see a 22-year-old on Instagram with a luxury watch and assume he's made it. You don't ask if it was bought on EMI. Or if it was borrowed. Or sponsored. Or a reward for a sacrifice you don't know about.

Comparison, when done blindly, is lethal.

This culture makes us chase lifestyles before we've even learned how to fund one. It makes us ashamed of being "low budget" instead of being proud of living within our means. It tricks us into measuring self-worth through spending, not saving. And that's a trap we're not warned about.

No One's Carrying a Financial Manual

Here's the truth: Everyone's faking it, at some level.

The guy in your class who always has the newest phone? Maybe he's stressed about his parents seeing the bill.

The girl who never says no to dinner plans? Maybe she's skipping breakfast to make up for it.

The influencer posting stock screenshots and "wealth-building" hacks? Maybe she's one bad decision away from being scammed.

Nobody's walking around with a financial instruction manual. But some are smart enough to write their own. That's what this book is about.

A Moment of Reflection

Pause. Think about the last financial decision you made:

- Was it planned?
- Was it pressure?
- Was it based on information or imitation?

If you hesitate to answer, don't worry. That's not failure. That's awareness. And awareness is the first step toward control.

No one expects you to know everything. But you owe it to yourself to start learning now. Not after you get your first job. Not when the debts pile up. Not when the guilt kicks in. Now. While you still have time, energy, and space to grow without the baggage.

Repeating the Cycle or Ending It

Let's not sugarcoat it: most of us grew up watching our parents either worry about money or hide their money issues completely. Either way, we didn't learn. We just absorbed anxiety. Or silence. Or both.

For a fact, financial ignorance is inherited. Parents didn't have this education either. Most learned about money the hard way, trial, error, regret, repeat. They were never shown what budgeting meant or how to invest early. So, they passed down what they knew: sacrifice, survival, and secrecy.

A generation that didn't get the tools is now raising a generation without direction. That's how financial ignorance becomes generational, not because anyone wants it to, but because no one knows how to break it.

And when children finally face the real world, armed with degrees but no financial sense, they flounder.

They think taking a loan is like getting free money. They think savings can wait. They think their first paycheck will fix everything. They think a better salary will solve what bad habits created.

Until life slaps them with interest rates, impulse debts, and the sobering weight of independence.

Now the question is: do we pass the same thing forward? Or do we stop the cycle?

Financial knowledge isn't a privilege anymore. It's a necessity. Like knowing how to drive or cook. It's something every 16 to 30-year-old should possess, not as an "extra" skill, but as part of their basic toolkit for life.

The fact that you're reading this means you're ready to build that toolkit. You've already taken the first step that most don't: caring enough to know.

Financial Literacy = Survival Literacy

Let's make one thing clear: Financial literacy is not optional anymore.

It's not something you learn "once you start earning." It's what prepares you to earn well, spend wisely, save regularly, and live peacefully.

And it's not about being good at math or being rich.

It's about knowing:

- How much is too much when spending on a friend's birthday.
- Why saving for a ₹3000 emergency matters more than owning a ₹30,000 watch.
- That just because something is "on offer" doesn't mean it's worth it.
- That "interest-free" doesn't mean free.
- That even ₹500 saved a month is better than ₹0.

In today's world, where consumerism screams louder than caution, where apps can drain your wallet faster than your mind can react, not knowing is dangerous.

Because the price isn't always financial. Sometimes it's your mental health, your relationships, your confidence, your dreams.

A Generation Built on Appearances

Scroll through Instagram or Snapchat, and you'll find 17-year-olds showing off shoes worth ₹20,000 and dining out like they're investment bankers. Scroll a bit more and you'll see someone showing off a vacation paid through credit, not clarity.

Likes become currency. Visibility becomes worth. And behind all that, authenticity fades.

This is the generation of screenshots, not savings. Of filters over facts. Of "how it looks" over "what it costs."

We don't need to blame social media; it's not the villain. But without the right foundation, it becomes a fast track to destruction. When you don't know how money really works, you assume everyone has it. And then you try to match lives you can't afford.

So you swipe. You borrow. You postpone bills. And you fall into traps others have already fallen into, just because nobody shared the behind-the-scenes.

From Comparison to Consequences

Let's revisit that story of the boy who got a fancy bike. He wanted what others had. He didn't know what his family could or couldn't truly afford. He thought owning it meant belonging.

But what it really meant was this:

- His father skipped repairing their leaking roof that month.
- His mother stopped going to her health checkups.
- Their monthly savings plan came to a halt.

That's how invisible costs work.

No one talks about them, but they shape real sacrifices.

He didn't mean harm, but not knowing the impact made him blind to the harm he caused.

This isn't to guilt anyone. It's to raise awareness. To tell you that your choices, especially financial ones, always ripple. Even when you think it's your money, your card, your life, it never really is. Not in a connected world. Not in an Indian household.

The Compass You Didn't Know You Needed

So, how do you fix this?

You start by treating financial literacy like any other survival skill. Like swimming. Or cooking. Or using Google Maps.

You don't wait until you're drowning to learn how to swim. You don't wait until you're starving to learn how to make dal. And you shouldn't wait until you're broke to learn how budgeting works.

This book is that compass. It's not about getting rich. It's about not getting lost.

It's about guiding you through:

- Knowing what you have.
- Understanding what you need.
- Spending without regret.
- Saving without struggle.
- Investing without fear.

And it starts right here, in this chapter. With your decision to not be clueless anymore.

A Wake-Up Call, Not a Scolding

Let this be clear: this chapter isn't here to scold you. It's here to wake you up.

You're not too young. You're not too broke. You're not too late.

You're exactly where you need to be, before the fall, before the panic, before the debt.

And the fact that you're reading this already puts you ahead of 90% of your peers who think they'll "figure it out later."

Later is a myth.

Now is where your power lies.

Why We're Not Waiting for a Crash Course

Imagine you're handed a vehicle at 18. It looks sleek. It moves fast. Everyone else seems to be cruising in theirs. There are no instructors, no signals, no maps. Just a key and a wink: "Figure it out. Everyone does eventually."

So you drive.

You skid on EMI corners. You crash into credit traps. You follow flashy cars without checking your own fuel.

By the time you learn how to drive, the damage has already been done.

This is how most people learn about money.

But here's a thought: What if you could get the map before the ride? What if you had someone tell you:

- Here's how you accelerate your income without losing control.
- Here's how you apply the brakes before going overboard.
- Here's how you change gears when life throws new challenges at you.

That's what this book is.

Not a lecture. Not a crash course. But a GPS for your financial life, starting now.

Start Small, But Start Now

You don't have to be a financial guru.

You don't need to be reading balance sheets or playing the stock market. You just need to begin with the basics:

- Know where your money comes from.
- Track where your money goes.

- Learn how to say no, even to yourself.
- Understand why that ₹200 Zomato order might feel good now, but leave you short later.

It's not about being rich. It's about being ready.

You could start with something as small as:

- Creating a weekly budget with just ₹500.
- Listing out 3 unnecessary expenses from last week.
- Asking your parents what your monthly home expenses roughly look like.

Each of these steps is a door. Once you walk through, the next one appears. And soon, you're building a mindset that doesn't panic at the mention of money, but plans, adapts, and thrives.

If You've Ever Thought This

Let's address some common thoughts you might have had: "But I don't have any money yet." Perfect. Then you won't have to unlearn bad habits.

"Isn't this too early to be thinking about savings and insurance?" Not really. Time is your biggest asset. Use it well, and you'll save 10x later.

"This sounds overwhelming. Where do I even begin?" With this book. With this chapter. With this sentence. Every expert was once a beginner. Every financially stable adult once asked, "What's a mutual fund?"

Lighting a Candle Instead of Cursing the Darkness

Maybe you're reading this with regret.

Maybe you've already made some bad decisions. Maybe your account is already overdrawn, your credit score has already dipped, and your guilt is already rising.

Here's your reminder: you're not too late.

Every day is a new budget. Every mistake is a better plan waiting to happen. Every ₹10 saved is a step forward.

You don't have to go from zero to millionaire. You just have to move from unaware to aware.

And that change starts right now, with the commitment to not let ignorance be your excuse anymore.

What This Book Will and Won't Do

Let's set some expectations.

This book won't promise you shortcuts to wealth. It won't throw jargon at you. It won't pretend to be a finance textbook in disguise.

What it will do is something far more useful.

It will teach you how to:

- Think clearly about money.
- Ask better questions before spending.
- Recognize traps that come disguised as offers.

- Build a financial identity that's rooted in reality, not trends.
- Set yourself up to live with freedom, not just income.

And more importantly, it'll help you stop fearing money conversations.

Because once you understand money, you'll no longer feel like you're chasing it. You'll walk beside it, with control, with calm, and with clarity.

Why This Isn't Just "Another Book"

There are many books about money out there. Some focus on investing. Some on getting rich. Some use graphs. Some use theories.

This one is different.

Because it doesn't just want you to get rich. It wants you to become financially sane.

There's a difference.

Being rich might mean driving a luxury car with loans stacked under the hood. Being financially sane means understanding that a second-hand scooter, bought without debt, gives you real freedom.

Being rich might mean having ₹2 lakhs in a credit limit and no idea how you'll repay it. Being financially sane means knowing you have ₹20,000 saved and sleeping peacefully at night.

This book is about you building a life where:

- You don't panic when rent is due.
- You don't fight over borrowed money.
- You don't scroll with jealousy.
- You don't live paycheck to paycheck.

It's about you being proud of saying, "Yes, I know my money. I respect it. And it respects me back."

If You Still Think Money is Boring

Let's be real. Finance can seem dry.

Budgeting? Yawn. Savings? Meh. Insurance? Zzz.

But what if I told you that every financial decision is a story? A decision about who you are and who you want to become.

That ₹150 coffee every day? It's not about the caffeine. It's about comfort. That EMI for the latest phone? It's not about specs. It's about status. That choice to skip insurance? Not about laziness. It's about not wanting to think about the future.

Every rupee you earn or spend tells a story about your values, your dreams, your fears.

This book helps you become the author of that story.

It helps you turn your money into a character that supports your plot, not hijack it.

Your Financial Life is Your First Business

Imagine treating your own life like a start-up. You've got:

- Limited capital (your pocket money, stipend, or salary).
- Resources to manage (time, energy, data plans, food, rent).
- Goals to hit (graduation, job, travel, independence).
- Unexpected setbacks (a medical bill, a broken phone, inflation).

If this were a company, would you run it without a plan?

Of course not. You'd strategize. So why should your personal finances be any different?

You are the CEO of your life. You have to understand your cash flow, your risks, your investments, and your backup plans.

This doesn't mean you become obsessed. It means you become aware.

And with awareness comes power. Not the kind that shows off, but the kind that sustains.

So What Now?

Read this book like your future depends on it, because it does.

Take it slow. Reflect. Try the exercises. Don't worry if you mess up the first few times. That's normal.

But keep coming back. Keep asking. Keep learning.

By the end of this journey, you'll walk away with more than knowledge. You'll walk away with a sense of ownership over your money story.

And that's something no mistake, no scam, no pressure, and no peer can take away from you.

Meera's Awareness

Meera, also 21, viewed money differently. Even while in college, she tracked her expenses in a simple notebook. She made small savings out of her stipend and took up freelance gigs to add to her income. By the time she landed her first job, she already knew how to manage rent, groceries, and savings. Her salary didn't shock her; it empowered her.

Meera's early awareness gave her stability. While Rahul was stressed, she felt confident. Her story shows why money matters at every stage; not later, but right now.

- Rahul drifted through life thinking money would sort itself out. When reality struck, he was unprepared, stressed, and dependent.
- Meera, on the other hand, built awareness early. Her calm confidence came not from having more money, but from respecting it sooner.

Lesson: You don't need to wait for a job or adulthood to take money seriously. Awareness is your first step toward independence.

Ask Yourself: Do you want to stumble into the financial world like Rahul, or step into it with clarity like Meera?

One Last Thought Before You Move to Chapter 2

You've probably heard the saying: "Money doesn't buy happiness."

Fair enough. But let's tweak that a bit: "Financial understanding prevents a lot of unhappiness."

And that's exactly what this chapter was for. To start your journey with awareness, not regret. With curiosity, not fear. With strength, not stress.

You've just taken the first step.

Now let's build the staircase, one chapter at a time.

Chapter 2: Money Habits Begin Early - How Financial Behavior Forms

Aniket's Blind Spots

Aniket grew up in a family where money was never discussed. His parents paid for everything: clothes, outings, and tuition. Whenever he asked about finances, he was told, "You'll understand when you're older."

When Aniket finally got his first job, he was lost. He had no clue about taxes, no habit of saving, and no sense of responsibility. Because money had always been "someone else's problem," he stumbled badly when it became his own.

The Invisible Beginnings of Money Behavior

Before we ever earn, budget, or invest, before we even hold our own debit card, our relationship with money has already begun. And not quietly, it begins loudly, under the surface.

Through what we see.

Through what we feel.

Through what we're told, or not told.

Money behavior isn't born when the first salary comes in. It's born in a hundred small moments that don't feel financial at all.

Watching a parent count cash behind a closed door.

Overhearing a fight about bills.

Being told, “We can’t afford that,” without understanding why.

Seeing a friend get something you wanted, and realizing you couldn’t have it.

These aren’t financial decisions, but they are financial lessons. Every moment where money was present, discussed, withheld, or demanded, we absorbed something. And those early impressions, unprocessed and unexamined, go on to become the foundation for how we treat money when it finally enters our hands.

Not with logic. With habit.

That’s why two people with the same income can end up living vastly different financial lives. Because while numbers matter, behavior runs the show.

Why Behavior Comes Before Budget

A common myth many young adults carry is this: “Once I start earning, I’ll figure it out.”

As if income magically brings discipline. As if adulthood somehow rewires our financial instincts.

But money doesn’t teach you how to use money.

Experience doesn’t automatically translate to wisdom.

And earning more doesn’t mean you’ll manage better.

Because the real driver isn’t income. It's the habit.

If your early conditioning taught you to chase instant gratification, then your salary will become fuel for that habit.

If you learned to avoid talking about money, you'll avoid looking at your bank balance.

If money were always tight, you might hoard it, fear it, or spend it recklessly just to feel a moment's relief.

The behavior comes before the budgeting. And if we want financial well-being later, we must look at the conditioning we carry from before we even touch money.

The Home as the First Finance Class

In most homes, money isn't discussed like math or science. It isn't taught. It's demonstrated.

Some households model frugality with pride, budgeting, planning, and discussing openly. Others model silence, tension, or avoidance.

Some families carry the weight of comparison. Others pass on the legacy of sacrifice.

And so, the first lessons don't come through formal advice. They come through osmosis.

A child who sees their parents stretch every rupee grows up believing money is scarce.

A teenager whose pocket money is given with guilt learns that spending is something to hide.

A young adult who's never allowed to ask questions grows up ashamed to talk about finances.

The result? We step into the real world financially unprepared, not because no one told us the rules, but because we were never invited to notice our starting line.

No two homes are the same. But what every home leaves behind is a set of invisible financial cues. And they stay with us much longer than we think.

Family Silence and Social Noise

While families often stay silent, the outside world doesn't.

Social influence begins early.

In school, status is signaled through gadgets and brands.

In college, it's the bike you ride or the places you eat.

Online, it's everything from travel reels to unboxing videos.

The message is clear: if you're not consuming, you're falling behind.

It's a dangerous distortion. Because behind every visible lifestyle, there's an invisible context:

- The person who's always ordering food delivery might be skipping meals to balance costs.
- The student with the latest laptop might be repaying a loan in quiet installments.
- The one posting photos from fancy cafes might be doing it for a side hustle or sponsorship, not leisure.

But all you see is the result. And without context, comparison becomes a habit.

This is where money behavior starts to take a turn. You're no longer spending on needs or joy. You're spending to catch up, to match a standard that might not even be real.

And in doing so, you shape your financial life not around your reality, but around other people's noise.

Understanding Financial Boundaries Early

The problem is never "wanting more." The problem is "not knowing where you're starting from."

Many young adults copy lifestyles without understanding the financial structure behind them.

A friend's budget may include parental support. Yours may not.

A peer may earn double than what you do.

A classmate may live rent-free.

When these things go unspoken, boundaries blur.

That's why families must talk openly about financial ability, not to limit ambition, but to create clarity. Children shouldn't grow up feeling ashamed of their situation. Nor should they grow up entitled, assuming anything they want can or will be given.

Financial maturity begins when you know your baseline, not to shrink your dreams, but to ground your behavior.

Only when you know your family's limits can you make responsible requests, respect what you have, and begin planning your path forward, on your own terms.

Why It's Not Just About "Being Good with Money"

A lot of people say, "I'm just not good with money." As if it's a personality flaw. Something you're born with or without.

But it's not about being good or bad. It's about being aware or unaware.

If you overspend when you're stressed, that's not because you're bad with money; it's because money became your coping mechanism.

If you avoid budgeting, it might be because you fear seeing the truth.

If you borrow from friends without planning repayment, it might be because you grew up never seeing debt talked about properly.

These aren't character flaws. They're behavioral imprints. And like any imprint, they can be redefined.

The first step is to stop blaming yourself. The next step is to get curious.

What drives my choices?

What triggers my spending?

What emotion am I trying to satisfy when I swipe, borrow, or click?

Once you ask those questions, behavior begins to change, naturally, not forcefully.

From Observation to Ownership

The gap between observation and ownership is everything.

You can't control what you were exposed to growing up.

You can't change how money was handled in your home or your early environment.

But you can choose to stop carrying that script forward.

You can learn to say, "That's what I saw, but it's not how I'll act."

You can question the story that tells you

- that spending is status,
- that asking questions is shameful,
- that earning is freedom to waste.

You can rewrite the emotional connection you have with money, from fear to clarity, from avoidance to awareness, from impulsive to intentional.

That shift doesn't come from income. It comes from introspection.

And it starts when you understand that your earliest money habits weren't about money at all. They were about emotions, environment, and survival.

Now, you get to make it about choice.

Peer Influence: When Money Becomes a Social Costume

At some point, financial decisions stop being just about money and start becoming about fitting in. That point often comes early, when belonging matters more than budgeting, and visibility feels more urgent than values.

Teenagers and young adults aren't always spending money to express themselves. More often, they're spending to avoid exclusion.

What starts as one friend suggesting a dinner plan becomes everyone agreeing silently, even if it means borrowing money.

What begins as a classmate showing off their new phone turns into a self-comparison spiral, not because you wanted the phone, but because you wanted what it represented: relevance.

No one says it aloud, but the social expectation is clear: if you can't keep up, you might get left out. So you don't say no. You swipe, borrow, or compromise quietly, not to indulge yourself, but to protect your place in the group.

The tragedy? That most people around you are doing the same.

The Silent Economics of Social Currency

Every peer group has its own unspoken currency. In some circles, it's clothes. In others, it's gadgets, cars, or travel stories. The specifics change. But the pressure stays the same.

What makes it more dangerous is the illusion of choice. On the surface, you're choosing to participate. But under the surface, you're being pulled by the fear of being seen as less.

This pressure forces many young people to:

- Spend before they're ready
- Buy things they don't care about
- Say yes to plans they can't afford
- Feel guilty for having boundaries

And in trying to "not look broke," they often break their budgets, and more painfully, their self-trust.

We rarely talk about the psychological toll of this constant performance. But it's real. Every time you make a financial decision based on what others expect, instead of what you can afford, you're trading clarity for acceptance.

Owning Your Financial Reality

One of the most liberating realizations in early adulthood is this: you're allowed to make decisions that align with your situation, even if they don't match your surroundings.

This doesn't mean giving up ambition. It means refusing to sabotage yourself for optics.

Everyone's starting line is different. Some people have a financial cushion. Some have constraints. Some were taught structure. Some are still figuring it out.

Pretending you're at the same point as everyone else doesn't get you closer. It only puts you at risk.

You don't need to explain your boundaries to anyone. But you do need to respect them yourself.

And once you do, the peer pressure fades. Not because it disappears, but because it no longer directs your behavior.

The First Line of Defense: Clarity

When you don't know your limits, you don't know when to say no.

That's why the first step to resisting unnecessary social spending isn't self-control. It's clarity.

Know your monthly range.

Know your goals.

Know what you're okay sacrificing and what you're not.

Once you have that, every decision, whether it's something as small as buying something for yourself or your friend or something as thoughtful as investing your money in something lucrative, becomes a conscious one.

Ask yourself:

- Is this choice aligned with what I value?
- Is it emotionally triggered or financially planned?
- Will it cost me more than just money?

These aren't philosophical questions. They're survival tools. And the earlier you ask them, the stronger your foundation becomes.

Spending Triggers: The Emotional Backdoor

Many of us think we spend because of logic, sales, need, or timing. But most spending is emotional. And the emotions come in quietly, in disguise.

You're not buying the new shoes because you need them. You're buying them because you feel behind.

You're not ordering food because there's nothing at home. You're doing it because you're stressed or bored.

You're not upgrading your phone because the old one is useless. You're doing it because the new one makes you feel more "in."

This is how most financial behavior unfolds, not from analysis, but from emotional autopilot. We feel something. We act. We justify after.

But if you can catch the emotion before the action, you change the entire script.

Delayed Gratification: More Than Just Waiting

Delayed gratification isn't about saying no. It's about learning to say "not now" with power.

Imagine wanting something badly, a gadget, a trip, a lifestyle change. Instead of reacting, you pause. You think. You plan. And you make the decision a week later, not out of impulse, but out of alignment.

This isn't about denying yourself. It's about preserving control.

In that pause, you learn what really matters. Sometimes, you still buy the thing. But now, it's a decision. Not a reflex.

That pause, however small, is where emotional maturity grows. And that's where real financial discipline is born, not from restriction, but from choice.

Identity Is Shaped by Repetition, Not One-Off Wins

If you've ever said, "I'm not disciplined," it's probably because you've messed up a few times.

Maybe you overspent.

Maybe you avoided your bank balance.

Maybe you forgot to repay a friend.

But none of these define you.

What defines you is what you repeat.

Your identity around money isn't built from a single mistake or a single good month. It's built from patterns. And patterns can be redesigned.

Start small:

- Set one rule for spending this week.
- Track one category of expense.
- Say no to one thing that doesn't serve you.

Every time you do this, you're teaching your brain something new: I don't have to act on every urge. I can create distance. I can choose differently.

And slowly, you start seeing yourself not as someone who struggles with money, but someone who's learning to lead with it.

From Emotion to Intention

Here's what no one tells you: financial growth doesn't feel dramatic. It feels quiet. Boring, even.

It's the choice to stay in instead of going out. The decision to postpone gratification. The 20-second pause before clicking 'buy now. ' The habit of tracking what you spent, even if it makes you uncomfortable.

There's no applause. No spotlight. Just a growing sense of calm. And that calm becomes your new center.

Eventually, money stops being something that controls you. It becomes something you understand. And then, something you direct.

That shift, from emotional reactivity to intentional clarity, is where behavior becomes freedom.

The Silence That Shapes Us

In many homes, money isn't a subject; it's a secret. Parents handle it privately. Children are expected to stay out of it. Questions are deflected or dismissed. The result? A generation that grows up around money without ever understanding how it works.

This silence may be well-intentioned. Perhaps parents want to protect their children from stress. Or they believe "they'll learn when they're older." But what gets protected doesn't get prepared. And what gets postponed rarely gets prioritized.

When money isn't discussed, we fill the gaps with guesses.

We assume.

We imagine.

We absorb random cues from the world around us.

And often, those cues lead us toward guilt, confusion, or entitlement.

When Kids Don't Know the Context

Without clarity, assumptions take over.

A child sees a relative buy a new car and assumes their family is falling behind.

A teenager notices that her parents never say "no" and assumes money will always be available.

A young adult, offered no insight into the family's real financial health, makes bold demands or unnecessary sacrifices without knowing which one is appropriate.

When families avoid the topic of money, they don't erase the questions. They simply leave them unanswered.

And those unanswered questions become the framework for future decisions, often poor ones.

The Entitlement Trap

Some families over-give. They stretch their limits to provide their children with the best, thinking they're doing them a favor. The child, seeing no sign of struggle, begins to assume that access is permanent. That things will always work out. That someone will always cover for them.

That belief, unspoken, unintended, is entitlement. And it sets the stage for reckless financial behavior later.

Not out of greed. Out of assumption.

When money has always arrived without explanation, its absence feels like betrayal. When spending has never had consequences, limits feel like punishment.

Breaking entitlement doesn't mean shaming kids. It means teaching you where the line is, and why it matters. It means saying, "This is what we can afford. This is what we're planning for. And this is what you'll need to handle on your own someday."

It's not a lecture. It's a gift.

Clarity Without Burden

There's a difference between understanding how money works and feeling responsible for it all.

Being aware of financial reality sounds like this:

- "Your family is saving for your education, and here's how it's being done."

- "This trip is happening because someone planned for it in advance."
- "We're skipping that expense this month to focus on something more important."

These kinds of messages help you see the logic behind choices. They show how decisions are made, how priorities work, and how planning makes things possible.

But sometimes, the way money is talked about can feel like pressure. That sounds more like:

- "Do you think money grows on trees?"
- "You're the reason things are always tight."
- "We're under a lot of stress because of your needs."

Those kinds of statements don't build awareness; they just leave you feeling guilty, even though the situation isn't your fault.

The goal isn't to make anyone feel bad about money. It's to help you see the connection between choices and consequences, so you can start building your own good habits.

And once that happens, something shifts. You begin to take ownership of how you think about money, and that's the kind of mindset that builds lifelong confidence.

Rewriting Financial Beliefs

We all inherit beliefs about money. Some are obvious. Others are invisible until they start affecting our decisions.

Common inherited beliefs include:

- "Money is stressful."
- "Talking about money is rude."
- "It's selfish to want too much."
- "Rich people are lucky, or corrupt."
- "If I have money, I should spend it fast, before it disappears."

Most of us never question these beliefs. We just operate within them. They shape how we view our worth, our future, and our limits.

But beliefs are not facts. They're interpretations. And they can be rewritten.

How Beliefs Become Behavior

Let's say you grew up believing that money equals freedom. That can motivate you to work hard, but it might also lead you to spend excessively the moment you have income, confusing spending with liberation.

Or maybe you believed money was unstable. That perception may cause you to be fearful, avoidant, or excessively stingy, even when you are doing well.

Beliefs shape the decisions, quietly, softly. That's why gaining awareness of them is potent.

Ask yourself:

- What did I learn about money from my family?
- What did they do well? What did they struggle with?
- Which of their behaviors have I copied without realizing it?

This isn't about blame. It's about reclaiming control. Once you see the belief clearly, you can choose a different one.

Build a New Money Story

You don't need to believe everything you inherited.

If you were taught that money is hard to keep, you can learn how to manage it better.

If you were shown that saving is fearful hoarding, you can reframe it as strategic planning.

If you grew up thinking you'll always be taken care of, you can develop the pride of becoming self-reliant.

Your story is still being written. And from this point on, you hold the pen.

One belief at a time, you can build a framework that supports your goals, instead of sabotaging them.

Small Habits That Shift the Narrative

You don't need a full financial overhaul to change course. You just need a few anchored behaviors that reinforce your new story.

Try this:

- Track one category of spending this month. Observe without judgment.
- Have one conversation with a family member about money, not to ask for anything, but to understand something.
- Delay one purchase you want, not because you can't afford it, but because you want to test your emotional attachment.

Each of these small acts chips away at the old pattern and begins creating a new one. Not dramatically. Quietly. Consistently.

And that's where lasting change lives, not in big declarations, but in small daily realignments.

Building Long-Term Leverage from Early Awareness

When you build awareness early, you don't just avoid mistakes; you gain leverage.

Leverage means you learn faster.

You recover quicker.

You see problems before they grow.

You make confident decisions instead of reactive ones.

And most importantly, you stop being afraid of money.

You start seeing it for what it is: a tool. A resource. A responsibility. Not a threat. Not a mystery. Not a test.

With awareness, money becomes something you work with, not something you fight against.

That shift is priceless. And it's possible at any age, but easiest when you start early.

Beyond Knowledge: Reinforcing Identity Through Behavior

Knowing how money works is helpful. But how you see yourself in relation to money is what ultimately guides your behavior.

This is where many people get stuck. They read articles, attend seminars, download budget apps, but nothing sticks. Why? Because their internal identity hasn't shifted.

If you believe you're careless, you'll keep acting that way, even when you try not to.

If you believe you're someone who "just can't save," you'll always find a way to overspend.

If you see yourself as dependent, you'll avoid financial independence even when you can reach it.

Changing your identity isn't about affirmations. It's about evidence. You build it through small wins, repeated, reinforced, and respected.

Build Belief With Behavior

Every time you:

- Say no to something you can't afford.

- Choose to plan instead of react.
- Track your money without fear or shame.

You're not just managing your money. You're rewriting the kind of person you believe you are.

That shift is subtle at first. But it snowballs.

The more consistent you become, the more confident you feel.

The more confident you feel, the more power you gain.

The more power you gain, the less money controls your identity.

Suddenly, it's not about being "good with money." It's about being aligned with your decisions.

That's maturity. That's freedom.

Practice, Not Perfection

One of the most dangerous myths around financial behavior is the idea that you have to get it all right from the beginning.

You don't.

In fact, expecting perfection often leads to paralysis. You make one mistake, and you spiral. You tell yourself it's hopeless. You stop trying.

But money management is a skill. Like fitness. Like writing. Like learning a new language.

You don't get better by waiting until you're perfect. You get better by starting, even when it's awkward, inconsistent, or slow.

Make a mistake? Learn from it.

Spent impulsively? Track it and understand why.

Missed a goal? Rework it and try again.

The goal is not flawlessness. The goal is momentum.

Focus on Systems, Not Willpower

Most people think financial success comes from self-control. But self-control fades. Systems don't.

Instead of relying on daily willpower, build routines that protect your future.

Try these:

- Auto-transfer 5–10% of your income into a separate savings account the moment it arrives.
- Use only one app to track all your spending, and set reminders weekly.
- Categorize your expenses into three folders: Essentials, Joy, and Impulse. At the end of each month, reflect on how balanced the picture looks.

These systems don't just organize your finances. They organize your mind. They reduce decision fatigue. They make good choices easy and poor choices inconvenient.

And over time, they train you to trust yourself with money, quietly, consistently.

Cultivate Emotional Distance From Money

A mistake many young people make is tying self-worth to money. When their finances look good, they feel confident. When they're low on funds, they feel ashamed or anxious.

This attachment is dangerous. It keeps you stuck in emotional turbulence.

The truth? Money is a neutral resource. It reflects decisions, but it doesn't define you.

Detaching your identity from your bank balance is powerful. It allows you to:

- Handle financial lows with grace.
- Avoid financial highs from inflating your ego.
- Make calm decisions instead of panic-driven ones.

The earlier you learn this, the more peace you'll feel, regardless of your income level.

Normalize Money Conversations

You can only grow in areas you're willing to talk about.

If money remains a taboo topic, you'll avoid feedback. You'll struggle silently. You'll make decisions in isolation and carry shame even when you don't need to.

Normalize discussing money with people you trust, not to show off, but to learn.

Ask your peers:

- How do you plan your monthly budget?

- What's one money mistake you've learned from?
- How do you set boundaries when you can't afford something?

These conversations turn money from a stressor into a shared skill. And they create a support system that can guide you for life.

One Decision at a Time

Rewriting your money behavior doesn't require a radical transformation. It requires repetition.

One aligned decision. Then another. Then another.

That's how it begins.

You don't need a miracle.

You don't need to wait for the perfect job or the next paycheck.

You don't need to "figure everything out" in one go.

All you need is the awareness that your habits started early, and the willingness to lead them consciously from here on.

Kavya's Early Learning

Kavya's parents weren't rich, but they included her in small financial decisions. At 17, she managed her own pocket money and sometimes chipped in for family groceries. Her parents explained how bills worked, why savings mattered, and even showed her their bank statements.

So, when Kavya started earning, she wasn't overwhelmed. She set up her savings account, planned her spending, and avoided unnecessary debt. The foundation laid at home shaped her confidence as an adult.

Aniket V/s Kavya - The Difference

- Aniket grew up shielded from financial realities and entered adulthood confused, unprepared, and dependent.
- Kavya, exposed to small lessons early on, transitioned smoothly into financial responsibility and confidence.

Lesson: The habits and attitudes you form now, whether by choice or by ignoring them, shape your future stability.

Ask Yourself: Will you carry Aniket's blind spots into your adult life, or build Kavya's clarity while you still have time?

Key Takeaways – Chapter Summary

1. Money behavior begins early, shaped by home, observation, and emotion.
2. Peer pressure and comparison can override financial clarity if left unexamined.
3. Emotional triggers often drive spending. Awareness is the first line of defense.
4. Family silence can create financial confusion; open conversations build context.
5. Inherited beliefs around money must be questioned, not blindly accepted.

6. Identity around money is reinforced through small, consistent behaviors, not grand gestures.
7. Habits matter more than income, because without structure, more money only multiplies chaos.

If you're under 25 and reading this, you've already done something most people never do: you've paused to ask: Why do I behave this way with money?

That question is powerful. Not because it brings immediate answers, but because it opens the door to long-term transformation.

You don't have to become a financial expert overnight. But you do have to become the kind of person who's willing to lead themselves.

Because money doesn't make you who you are. But who you are will always determine what you do with your money.

And that's the real beginning of financial freedom.

Chapter 3: Financial Fumbles - Mistakes Youngsters Commonly Make

Siddharth's Spiral

Siddharth, 22, landed his first job and celebrated with a credit card. At first, it felt like free money - weekend trips, fancy clothes, and gadgets. Peer pressure made him spend even more. Soon, he was juggling three cards, paying only minimum balances, and taking out small online loans to keep up.

Within a year, Siddharth's debts outweighed his salary. Calls from lenders became daily torture. What started as fun quickly spiraled into financial stress.

The Age of Earning, The Era of Errors

Money doesn't come with an instruction manual. Most young adults step into financial independence through trial and error. The unfortunate part? The errors often cost more than just money; they cost momentum, mental peace, and in some cases, even future stability.

What's worse is that these financial missteps are not rare exceptions. They're patterns, recurring themes among young people from every background.

Why? Because the modern world throws complex financial tools and temptations at young minds before they've developed the clarity to handle them. And when information is lacking, mistakes are inevitable.

But here's the good news: mistakes can be prevented if you know what they look like.

This chapter is a mirror. It reflects the most common money traps that young people fall into. Not to shame, but to sharpen your awareness. If even one of these patterns sounds familiar, it's not a reason to panic. It's a reason to pause, reflect, and pivot.

Let's start with the ten most common financial fumbles that define early adulthood.

1. Reckless Spending: The Instant Gratification Spiral

The first taste of independence often comes with a paycheck. But with it comes something sneakier, impulse.

The moment money lands in the account, the urge to spend kicks in. New gadgets. Weekend getaways. Branded clothes. Upgraded memberships. There's a strange, almost celebratory sense of "I've earned this," followed by purchases that weren't even on the radar a day earlier.

The core mistake here isn't spending; it's spending without strategy.

The problem isn't indulgence. It's unconsciousness. Buying without planning, tracking, or pausing. When left unchecked, this quickly turns into paycheck-to-paycheck survival, even when the paycheck is decent.

And no, it's not just a "youngster problem." It's a behavioral loop. The earlier you catch it, the easier it is to break.

2. Blind Investing: Playing Grown-Up Without Knowing the Game

Investing is a powerful tool. But only when you know what you're doing. Today, however, the investing world has become a loud performance arena. People are buying stocks, cryptocurrencies, IPOs, and mutual funds not out of understanding, but out of FOMO.

Platforms make it look easy. "Just one tap and you're a shareholder." But the mistake isn't the technology, it's the misuse of access.

Blind investing is when someone:

- Buys stock because a friend said it "will double soon."
- Puts money into a trendy coin because it's "the future."
- Chooses an investment just because the app shows it's "popular this week."

Without understanding the business, the risk, or the timeline, young people enter markets emotionally and exit painfully.

Real investing begins with education. Without it, you're not building wealth; you're gambling in disguise.

3. The Social Spending Trap: Buying to Belong

Peer pressure doesn't end after school. It just gets more expensive.

A colleague flaunts their new smartwatch. A friend group books a weekend resort stay. Your flatmate upgrades to the latest iPhone.

You don't want to be left behind, not just in stuff, but in social identity. So, you join in.

But here's the truth most won't say: many people are spending to keep up appearances, not because they can afford it.

This trap is especially dangerous because it disguises itself as "participation." You say yes to every plan. Swipe for every dinner. Click "buy now" just to feel like you're in sync.

Soon, your money isn't serving you. It's serving an invisible scoreboard. And you don't even know who's keeping score.

The cure? Discomfort. Learning to say, "That doesn't fit my budget right now."

It sounds awkward at first, but it's also the fastest way to take back control.

4. The "Quick Money" Mirage: Falling for Get-Rich-Quick Schemes

If there's one thing that consistently seduces young people, it's the promise of fast success.

From "double your money in a week" trading signals, to side hustles that promise passive income with zero effort, to influencers flexing their "earnings" from forex trading apps, it's everywhere.

What many don't see is the fine print. Or the legal loopholes. Or the mountain of people who lost everything trying to mimic someone else's shortcut.

Some get pulled into:

- High-risk crypto schemes with no transparency.
- Sports betting or online gambling disguised as "strategy."
- Paid courses that teach nothing but charge everything.
- MLM-style digital projects selling dreams, not returns.

The lure of quick money is strong. But the question to always ask is: "If it's that easy, why isn't everyone rich already?"

Behind most success stories is time, effort, failure, and iteration. Behind most quick-money traps is a con.

5. Misusing Credit Cards: Spending the Future Before It Arrives

A swipe here. A small EMI there. A few points earned. A cashback offer too good to miss.

And before you know it, you're drowning in revolving debt.

Credit cards, when used responsibly, can offer flexibility and even benefits. But for most young adults, they become a way to live above their means today, by borrowing from tomorrow.

The danger lies in how easy it feels:

- You're not "spending money." You're just using a card.
- The full repayment isn't due today, so it doesn't feel urgent.

- The minimum due feels manageable until the interest snowballs.

This mindset creates a dangerous illusion: that the money isn't real.

But it is. And the longer you avoid reality, the deeper the hole becomes.

Credit isn't evil. But credit without discipline is a trap. And no cashback is worth the cost of losing your peace.

6. Buy Now, Pain Later: BNPL and Instant Gratification Apps

The new generation of credit isn't even a card anymore. It's apps that say:

- "Split in 3 easy EMIs."
- "Buy now, pay in 15 days."
- "No-cost, no-worries shopping."

Sounds harmless. But these tools are debt in disguise.

Buy Now Pay Later platforms market themselves as friendly, interest-free helpers. But behind the scenes:

- They feed impulsive behavior.
- They make you feel like you're managing money better when you're just postponing discomfort.
- They often carry hidden penalties, delays, or penalties for late payments.

Worse, they normalize debt as a lifestyle. You begin to associate delay with control when it's really avoidance.

True affordability isn't whether you can defer payment. It's whether you could've paid upfront without hurting your plans.

If the answer is no, you're not buying within your means. You're just decorating your trap.

7. The Dependency Dilemma: Relying on Parents Too Long

Financial support from parents during student years or transitional phases is understandable. But when it stretches into years of working life, it quietly morphs into a problem, dependency disguised as convenience.

Some young adults live rent-free even after landing a job. Others keep expecting their parents to handle emergencies, bills, or even travel costs. In some cases, the salary goes entirely toward personal wants, while the needs are still parent-funded.

The issue isn't laziness, it's conditioning.

When support becomes default, independence becomes optional. And that optionality weakens the drive to manage money mindfully.

Here's what rarely gets discussed: Behind every extended dependency, there's a parent delaying their retirement.

A mother skipping health check-ups.

A father still working overtime.

An invisible sacrifice so the child doesn't have to feel discomfort.

It's not about guilt-tripping. It's about awakening.

True adulthood starts when you ask: Am I a contributor to my family's future or a continued consumer of its past security?

8. The "EMI = Affordability" Illusion

A message has been successfully planted into the minds of modern youth: If the EMI fits, you can afford it.

That's not just flawed, it's financially dangerous.

Equated Monthly Installments (EMIs) make large purchases look small. A ₹75,000 phone doesn't feel like a dent if you're paying ₹3,000 a month. But what's often ignored:

- The cost of interest over time
- The burden of overlapping EMIs from multiple purchases
- The psychological shift from ownership to obligation

Young people often juggle EMIs for:

- Phones
- Bikes
- Laptops
- Online courses
- Vacations

Individually, each EMI seems harmless. Together, they consume a major chunk of future cash flow, limiting flexibility and increasing stress.

Worse, this mindset stunts financial growth. Instead of saving and earning towards a goal, gratification becomes borrowed, and progress gets postponed.

Real affordability isn't about whether an EMI fits today. It's about whether the full cost aligns with your life goals over time.

9. The Lifestyle Creep: Upgrading Without Intention

You get a raise. You move to a better job. You start earning more. Naturally, you think, it's time to upgrade.

Better house. Better clothes. Better everything.

This is lifestyle creep, the slow, almost invisible expansion of expenses as income grows. And it's one of the biggest reasons young adults with decent salaries still feel broke.

The mistake here isn't wanting more. It's automating your upgrades without intention.

With every income increase, there should be a moment of pause:

- What do I need to improve?
- What am I upgrading just to signal status?
- How much of this extra money is going toward savings or investments?

If that pause doesn't happen, the upgrades become default. And soon, your cost of living catches up to your income. There's no room to breathe. No savings. No cushion.

It's not about avoiding luxury. It's about choosing it, consciously, strategically.

10. Ignoring Emergency Funds and Insurance

When you're young and healthy, the idea of preparing for emergencies seems boring, unnecessary, even pessimistic. But financial maturity isn't about reacting to life. It's about being ready for it.

A medical emergency. A job loss. A sudden home expense. An accident on a road trip.

Life rarely sends warnings. And when you're unprepared, it doesn't just cost money, it costs time, confidence, and momentum.

The two most common mistakes here are:

- Not having an emergency fund: No buffer to fall back on means every crisis becomes a financial disaster. Even a ₹20,000 emergency can derail your month.
- Ignoring insurance: Not getting health insurance early means paying higher premiums later, or worse, bearing massive hospital bills out of pocket. Similarly, avoiding term insurance leaves your family exposed if something unexpected happens.

Smart finances aren't just about wealth. They're about resilience. And nothing builds resilience like planning for the worst, even when you're at your best.

Real Stories, Real Lessons

Sometimes, the best way to understand a financial mistake is to hear how someone else lived through it. Not theoretical. Not abstract. But real, raw, and relatable.

Story 1: The Impulsive Investor

Arjun, 23, joined a new fintech startup straight out of engineering college. First salary in hand, he poured ₹40,000 into a hyped crypto coin his colleague swore would "triple in a month." It tanked in three weeks.

What he learned: "I thought I was investing. I was actually gambling, just with a better interface."

Today, he reads annual reports before putting even ₹1,000 into any company.

Story 2: The EMI Juggler

Sneha, 26, was living in a metro city, with EMIs on her laptop, scooter, phone, and a solo trip abroad, all running simultaneously. Her take-home pay was ₹52,000. Her EMIs totaled ₹29,000.

What she learned: "I wasn't living life, I was repaying it in installments."

She has since sold her scooter, switched to public transport, and started building her savings.

Story 3: The Late Realizer

Farhan, 29, lost his job during a market slowdown. He had no savings and no insurance. With parents retired and rent due, he borrowed from four friends and took a personal loan.

What he learned: "Stability isn't about your salary, it's about what you've saved and safeguarded."

Now, even in his new job, he lives two steps below his means and has built a six-month emergency fund.

These are not exceptions. They are reflections of what many silently go through.

If you find pieces of yourself in these stories, remember: you're not behind. You're just becoming aware. And that awareness is your most valuable financial asset.

How Small Mistakes Multiply Quietly

Most financial mistakes don't shout. They whisper.

One delayed bill.

One unplanned EMI.

One impulse purchase justified as a "reward."

One month of skipping savings "just this once."

Individually, they feel harmless. Almost rational. But the problem is not in the act, it's in the pattern.

Because once a behavior is normalized, it grows in the dark.

Let's take a ₹3,000 impulse spend. If it happens once, it's fine. If it happens monthly, that's ₹36,000 a year. Over five years, that's ₹1.8 lakh that could've earned interest, built savings, or helped in a crisis.

That's the dangerous part: the cost of inaction often shows up years later, by which time the habit feels cemented.

What begins as a small misstep becomes a lifestyle. And by the time it's visible, it's harder to reverse.

The Stories We Tell Ourselves

What keeps these patterns going isn't a lack of knowledge. It's the excuses we invent to protect our current behavior.

Here are some of the most common rationalizations:

- "I'll save once I start earning more."
- "Everyone my age is doing this."
- "Life is short, I deserve to enjoy now."
- "This is temporary; I'll fix it later."
- "I don't earn enough to make a difference anyway."

These aren't truths. They're stories, designed to avoid discomfort. Because change requires friction. And friction is uncomfortable.

But here's what most people don't realize: The discomfort of discipline today is far easier than the regret of chaos tomorrow.

Financial fumbles don't ruin lives in a day. They erode them silently, over time, through unchecked habits and convenient narratives.

The Denial Loop: Why We Avoid Looking at the Numbers

One of the most telling signs of financial misalignment is avoidance.

- You stop checking your bank balance.
- You don't open loan statements.
- You don't track your spending, not because you can't, but because you don't want to face the reality.

This is what psychologists call avoidance coping, choosing not to look, because looking would mean taking responsibility.

But avoidance doesn't protect you. It just delays pain.

And the longer you delay, the more drastic the solution has to be.

Facing your financial truth isn't a punishment; it's the first act of self-respect.

Even if it's messy. Even if the numbers scare you. Especially then.

Because once you face it, you can fix it.

The Emotional Cost of Repeated Mistakes

We often talk about the financial consequences of poor money behavior, debt, lack of savings, and missed opportunities.

But what about the emotional consequences?

- The anxiety of always being one unexpected bill away from panic.
- The shame of borrowing from friends, again.
- The guilt of depending on parents when you know you shouldn't.
- The regret of looking back and realizing how much money was wasted.

These emotions accumulate. They become part of your self-image. And over time, they eat into your confidence, which is harder to rebuild than money.

That's why correcting financial mistakes isn't just about getting richer. It's about restoring your sense of control.

Mindset Shifts That Break the Cycle

Correcting the course doesn't begin with tactics. It begins with thought patterns.

Here are five mindset shifts that help break the loop of repeated mistakes:

1. From "I'll save later" to "I'll start small now."

Waiting for a perfect moment only delays growth. Even ₹500/month builds momentum. Small steps create financial muscle.

2. From "I can't afford this lifestyle" to "This lifestyle doesn't align with my goals."

It's not about lack. It's about clarity. If it doesn't serve your future, it's not a loss; it's liberation.

3. From "I'm not good with money" to "I'm learning how to manage my finances."

This shift changes your identity from passive victim to active learner. And learners always improve.

4. From "Money is stressful" to "Money is manageable when faced with honesty."

Avoidance creates drama. Clarity breeds calm.

5. From "I'm behind" to "I'm getting back on track."

Guilt is heavy. Progress is light. Choose the frame that moves you forward.

The Role of Accountability

Change becomes easier when someone's watching, not to judge, but to support.

Accountability can take many forms:

- A friend with whom you discuss goals every month.
- A money tracker where you log daily expenses.
- A calendar reminder to review your bank balance weekly.
- A budgeting tool that sends weekly nudges.

It's not about control. Rather, it is about being conscious.

When you take accountability for your actions, you don't fall into impulse. Instead, you become more intentional. You pause. You weigh. You rethink.

And as you keep practicing that, you stop the cycle of mistakes, not because you have become perfect, but because you have become attentive.

Replacing Old Habits With Stronger Anchors

You can't remove a habit without replacing it. So instead of trying to "stop spending," build new anchors that feel rewarding.

Examples:

- Replace late-night shopping with a budgeting review + savings tracker update.
- Replace weekend mall trips with free local events or meet-ups that don't involve purchases.
- Replace food delivery temptations with cooking challenges (set a monthly savings target from skipped orders).

Make your money habits enjoyable, not punishments. Fun isn't the enemy of discipline, it's its strongest ally.

The Power of Forgiving Yourself

Lastly, and most importantly, you are allowed to have made mistakes.

There is no perfect financial journey. Everyone you admire for being financially stable has a backstory filled with errors, panic, missed EMIs, bad calls, and messy phases.

What matters is not how clean your past looks. What matters is how consciously you move forward.

Don't dwell. Don't replay the regret tape.

Learn. Adjust. Forgive. And act.

Because every financial comeback story begins with a simple decision: "I've had enough of this pattern. It ends now."

Correcting Course: Practical Fixes for Common Mistakes

Mistake 1: Reckless Spending

Fix: Use the Three-Bucket System for every paycheck.

- 60% for needs
- 30% for wants
- 10% for goals (savings/investments)

Track expenses weekly using one app; don't wait till the month ends. Seeing your spending in real-time changes how you approach money.

Mistake 2: Blind Investing

Fix: Follow the 90-Day Rule.

Don't invest in anything you don't understand after 90 days of reading, listening, and asking questions. Subscribe to one credible financial news source. Understand key terms such as risk appetite, time horizon, and diversification. Only invest once you can explain the product to a friend in simple words.

Mistake 3: Buying to Belong

Fix: Build your Personal Financial Identity.

Before every major non-essential expense, ask:

- "Would I buy this if no one knew I had it?"
- "Is this decision a reflection of my values or my surroundings?"

Being selective builds pride faster than being seen. The strongest financial identity is one that's rooted in self-awareness.

Mistake 4: Quick Money Traps

Fix: Use the Skeptic Filter.

Every time you hear about a "no-effort, high-return" opportunity, ask:

- "Who profits if I join?"
- "Where's the source of truth?"
- "Has this been verified independently?"

If it sounds too good to be true, it's built on your curiosity, not your interest.

Mistake 5: Credit Card Misuse

Fix: Treat your credit card like a debit card with a 30-day delay. Never spend what you can't repay in full by the due date. Set an auto-payment of the entire bill, not just the minimum due. Use cards only when there's a direct benefit (points, cashback) and you were going to make the purchase anyway.

Mistake 6: Buy Now, Pay Later

Fix: Use BNPL only for planned essentials, never for wants. Set a maximum of one active BNPL transaction at a time. Delay gratification by 24 hours on all BNPL temptations. If you still want it after a day, reassess if you need it.

Mistake 7: Parental Dependency

Fix: Set a transition timeline. If you're earning, take full ownership of one living expense within 30 days, rent, groceries, phone bill, etc. Gradually shift other costs every quarter. Share your plan with your parents; they'll often support it more than you assume.

Mistake 8: EMI = Affordability Myth

Fix: Use the Ownership Readiness Check. Before any EMI-based purchase, ask:

- "Would I still want this if I had to save and pay in full first?"
- "Is this a want or a need?"

Build the discipline to delay. It sharpens judgment like nothing else.

Mistake 9: Lifestyle Creep

Fix: Create an Income Growth Split Formula. For every ₹1,000 increase in salary:

- Save ₹500
- Invest ₹300
- Spend ₹200

Upgrades should be intentional, not automatic.

Mistake 10: Ignoring Emergency Planning

Fix: Build an Emergency Fund worth 3-6 months of essential expenses. Park it in a separate high-liquidity savings account. Automate contributions to it just like a subscription. It's the most underrated form of peace.

One Mistake Is Not Your Identity

Financial fumbles often make people feel ashamed. But that shame isn't useful unless it turns into movement.

You are not your past purchase.

You are not your overdue EMI.

You are not the regret of that missed investment.

You are someone who is becoming financially intelligent because you're now aware. And that alone sets you apart.

The real danger isn't the mistake, it's pretending it didn't happen.

The real failure isn't a poor choice, it's repeating it because it's familiar.

As long as you're reflecting, learning, and adjusting, you're winning.

Start With One Shift

Don't try to overhaul everything at once. That only leads to burnout or backlash. Instead, start with one financial correction from this chapter.

Just one:

- Maybe it's deleting that unused BNPL app.
- Or setting a weekly spending limit.
- Or calling your parents and telling them you'll take over your phone bill from now on.

One shift is enough to change momentum. And momentum builds discipline faster than motivation ever will.

Write Your New Financial Narrative

Imagine your future self-five years from now. Confident. Independent. Calm around money.

Now ask:

- What did they stop doing?
- What did they begin to track?
- What did they unlearn that you're still holding onto?

That version of you is already possible. This chapter is the handshake between the current you and the future you. A meeting point between awareness and action.

You've seen the traps. You've understood the patterns. Now it's your move.

Nisha's Discipline

Nisha, the same age as Siddharth, handled her first salary differently. She used a budget app to track spending and avoided credit cards until she built savings. She resisted FOMO when friends bought the latest phones and instead saved for her own travel goals.

Nisha wasn't "richer" than Siddharth, but she was debt-free, stress-free, and steadily building wealth. Her discipline made her financially secure while Siddharth struggled to escape mistakes.

- Siddharth chased appearances, debt, and impulsive thrills, only to find himself trapped.
- Nisha chose discipline, avoided quick-money traps, and built peace of mind.

Lesson: Mistakes in money multiply fast, but so do smart habits. One path leads to sleepless nights, the other to quiet confidence.

Ask Yourself: Do you want Siddharth's stress, or Nisha's stability?

Final Reflections

Let's be honest, money mistakes will still happen. Even the best financial minds take a few wrong turns.

But from now on, you'll never again walk into one blindly.

Because now you know:

- The signs
- The psychology
- The consequences
- And most importantly, the corrections

The real win is not in being mistake-free. The real win is in never making the same mistake twice. Your financial behavior doesn't need to be flawless. It just needs to be awake.

Chapter 4: Real Money, Real Decisions - From Pocket Money to Paychecks - The Shift No One Prepares You For

Varun's Disappointment

Varun always assumed his first job would bring endless freedom. He imagined a huge paycheck, stylish clothes, and weekends out. But when his salary arrived, the numbers shocked him. After deductions, PF, and taxes, his take-home was far less than expected. Rent, commute, and EMIs ate up most of it.

Worse, Varun couldn't say no when friends or relatives asked for money as he wanted to look generous. With no budget or boundaries, he ended up broke within two weeks of payday. His dreams of independence quickly turned into disillusionment.

The Unseen Line Between Pocket Money and Paychecks

For years, your relationship with money has been simple: you receive it. Sometimes from parents. Sometimes from relatives. Occasionally, from birthdays or festivals. It lands in your hands without expectation, without scrutiny, without strings.

You spend it freely. You save it sporadically. You worry about it only when you run out.

Then, something changes.

You get your first stipend. Your first freelance gig. Your first paycheck.

Suddenly, it's no longer "received money", it's earned money. And without warning, the rules shift.

Now there's pressure. Now there's planning. Now there are deductions, documentation, and decisions you've never faced before.

This transition, from pocket money to paychecks, isn't just a financial leap. It's a psychological one. And most people are unprepared for what it really demands.

Why This Transition Feels Bigger Than It Looks

When you start earning, even modestly, something fundamental changes: You become financially accountable to yourself.

It's no longer someone else's responsibility to cover your needs or bail you out. You're not just spending from a fixed allowance, you're spending from your own output.

That means:

- Every rupee earned carries emotional weight.
- Every expense now feels like a trade-off.
- Every decision reflects who you are becoming, not just what you want.

The transition isn't just about money.

It's about identity. Responsibility. Boundaries.

And if you don't navigate it intentionally, it becomes overwhelming very quickly.

What Earning Actually Does to Your Mindset

Most people assume that earning brings confidence, and yes, it can. But it also brings confusion, especially early on.

Here's why:

1. You overestimate your income. The number you get offered (CTC) isn't what hits your account.
2. You underestimate your expenses. Small, routine costs (subscriptions, transport, food, apps) pile up fast.
3. You struggle to say 'no.' Now that you earn, others expect you to contribute, treat, or spend more.
4. You feel guilty for enjoying money. Especially if your parents worked hard, you might hesitate to spend on yourself.
5. You fear responsibility. Bills, taxes, long-term planning, it all arrives without a guidebook.

Earning is supposed to feel empowering. But for many, it starts off feeling like pressure in disguise.

Unless you're equipped to handle it, that pressure turns into poor choices, burnout, or emotional disconnect from your own money.

Case in Point: Two Friends, One First Job

Take the story of two 23-year-olds, Raghav and Zubin.

Both graduated with engineering degrees. Both landed campus jobs with similar salaries. But within six months, their financial behavior looked completely different.

Raghav:

- Treated his first paycheck like a lottery win.
- Took on a phone EMI, subscribed to three OTT platforms, and started eating out five times a week.
- By the third month, he had borrowed from friends to make rent.

Zubin:

- Created a basic spreadsheet to track income vs. spending.
- Took his parents out for dinner after his first salary, but avoided big purchases.
- Set aside ₹2,000 every month for emergency savings.

Same income. Same start. Different paths.

What separated them wasn't intelligence. It was intention.

What Nobody Tells You About Your First Paycheck

The moment your first salary hits your account, it feels euphoric. But euphoria is short-lived, especially once reality kicks in.

Here's what you need to know right at the start:

1. Your salary ≠ Your take-home pay

The number on your offer letter (Cost to Company or CTC) includes things you won't see for months, or ever. Taxes, Employee Provident Fund (EPF), health insurance, gratuity, all of these get deducted upfront.

If your CTC is ₹4.8 lakh per year, don't expect ₹40,000/month in your account. Expect closer to ₹32,000-₹34,000, depending on how your company structures the package.

2. Taxes begin earlier than you think

Once you cross the basic exemption limit (currently ₹4 lakh for most), you're taxable. You may not feel it in the first year, but by the time bonuses or hikes come in, taxes become real. Learn early how to read a salary slip. It'll help you make sense of deductions and plan smarter.

3. EPF is not a deduction; it's a delayed bonus

Your EPF contribution is a forced savings plan. While it reduces your take-home pay today, it builds a retirement safety net. Don't view it as a loss. It's a quiet wealth builder, earning interest without your effort.

4. Cost of living isn't fixed

Whether you live with parents or independently, expenses tend to rise with income. New city? Add transport, rent, and utilities. New job? Add clothing, food, travel, and socializing. Tracking these is not optional; it's survival.

Understanding these basics early gives you an edge most first-jobbers don't have.

Learning to Track, Spend, and Save: Your First Real System

You don't need a complicated app. You don't need to become a budgeting wizard. You just need a simple, repeatable system.

Here's a practical model for anyone starting out:

1. Track Before You Budget

For the first 30 days of your job, don't try to budget. Just observe. Track every expense. Don't judge yourself, just note it down.

Patterns will emerge:

- Where your money leaks
- What your unconscious habits are
- What expenses give you joy vs. guilt

Awareness always comes before alignment.

2. Build the 50-30-20 Split (with flexibility)

A starting formula:

- 50% for needs (rent, transport, groceries, utilities)
- 30% for wants (entertainment, outings, shopping)
- 20% for goals (savings, investments, insurance)

If your salary is modest, these ratios can flex. But the structure teaches discipline.

3. Automate your goals

Manual savings don't work long-term. Auto-debit a fixed amount into a separate account the moment your salary arrives.

Treat savings like a non-negotiable bill, not a leftover. That mindset shift is key.

Building Boundaries with Yourself

Earning money brings freedom, but freedom without boundaries becomes chaos.

You must learn to say:

- "I can afford this, but I'm choosing not to right now."
- "Just because I earn doesn't mean I owe everyone."
- "I don't need to prove my adulthood by spending."

Set your own limits on:

- How often you eat out
- What percentage of income goes to fun vs. growth
- When it's okay to say no to friends, family, or peers

The hardest boundary? Saying no to yourself.

But that boundary is what creates long-term confidence.

Building Financial Boundaries with Others

When you start earning, it's not just your money that changes; your relationships change too.

Suddenly, your friends expect you to split the bill evenly, regardless of your salary difference.

Your younger cousin asks for help with fees.

Your sibling jokes about borrowing money for a phone upgrade.

Your parents hint at how proud they'd be if you started contributing at home.

And you? You feel torn.

You want to help. You want to be generous. But you also don't want to feel drained or manipulated.

This is where financial boundaries matter, not just with yourself, but with others too.

Why Boundaries Feel Awkward (But Are Necessary)

Setting money boundaries can feel cold or selfish, especially in India, where families are tightly interwoven and expectations are often unspoken.

But here's the truth: Saying "yes" to everyone is the fastest way to go broke and burn out.

If you don't protect your financial space, others will walk all over it, without even realizing they're doing it.

Boundaries are not about rejecting people. They're about choosing sustainability over social pressure.

They help you:

- Avoid resentment

- Stay focused on long-term goals
- Preserve generosity for when it truly matters

Three Boundaries Every Young Earner Needs to Define

1. The "Treat Culture" Line

Just because you've started earning doesn't mean you owe everyone a party. You can celebrate your first salary without feeling pressured to splurge.

Better version:

- Set a limit: "I'll celebrate within ₹1,000."
- Choose intentionality: "I'll treat only my closest two people."

Real friends respect your limits. Those who don't were just waiting for your paycheck.

2. The Family Support Frame

You don't have to contribute from day one. But you also shouldn't avoid it forever.

Discuss openly:

- What help is needed?
- What are you comfortable committing to?
- Whether it's monthly, occasional, or situational?

Be clear. Not vague. Vague commitments create confusion and guilt.

3. The Loan-to-Friend Rule

Set a personal rule: "I only lend what I can afford to never get back."

If it comes back, great. If it doesn't, you're not bitter or broken.

You're not a bank. You're a young adult trying to build stability. Own that truth.

From Internships to Income: Why Early Work Matters

One of the biggest myths that holds young Indians back is this: "You only start working after graduation."

That mindset is outdated and expensive.

Internships, part-time jobs, freelancing, volunteering, these are not just "extra" things. They are early muscles of independence.

Every hour spent working early does two things:

1. Gives you experience before experience is expected
2. Teaches you the value of effort before ego sets in

It's not about earning big. It's about learning how to earn.

Breaking the Stigma Around Early Earning

In many households, working before graduation is seen as a "distraction."

In others, it's treated as unnecessary if the family can provide.

But the world has changed.

Today, some of the most skilled professionals started by:

- Editing videos for creators during college
- Tutoring students online on weekends
- Selling crafts on Instagram
- Running a newsletter or blog
- Interning with startups during breaks

These aren't "side hustles."

They're confidence accelerators.

And yet, too many students hesitate. Not because they lack talent. But because they fear judgment.

Let's dismantle that.

Real Story: How a ₹5,000 Gig Changed Arushi's Life

Arushi, a 20-year-old English literature student, was curious about writing but unsure about making it a career. She landed a one-month content internship paying ₹5,000.

What she learned:

- How to meet deadlines
- How to take feedback
- How to write for readers, not professors

That small internship led to a part-time content role, which helped her land a better job after graduation.

Her words: "The money was nice. But the mindset shift was priceless. I stopped seeing myself as a student and started feeling like a contributor."

Early work is less about income and more about identity.

Financial Contribution at Home: A Quiet Act of Maturity

In many Indian families, the moment a child earns, parents say, "Keep your money, you've worked hard for it."

And that's beautiful. But here's the other side: Even if your parents don't ask, offering to contribute, even in small ways, is a mark of maturity.

It could be:

- Covering your own recharge
- Chipping in for groceries
- Buying dad, a new wallet
- Paying your own transport costs

These are small gestures. But they signal growth. They say: "I see what you've done for me. Let me return a little now."

It's not about money. It's about awareness.

And awareness builds trust faster than money ever will.

Self-Reliance vs. Entitlement: Redefining the Indian Youth Narrative

In urban India today, there are two parallel realities:

1. A growing wave of young professionals becoming financially aware, taking charge, and building independent lives.
2. An equally visible group still dependent on their parents for rent, bills, decisions, and even luxuries, well into their late 20s.

This isn't about blame. It's about culture.

For years, Indian families have shielded their children from financial struggle, sometimes too much.

The result?

Entitlement that feels like normalcy.

It shows up as:

- Expecting your parents to fund every new purchase
- Treating their support as a right, not a privilege
- Resisting responsibility because "they'll handle it"

This mindset is quietly dangerous. Because it doesn't just delay independence, it kills it.

Self-Reliance Is a Practice, Not a Declaration

You don't become self-reliant overnight. It's not a switch, it's a process.

Start by asking:

- Am I paying for my lifestyle, or is someone else still cushioning me?
- Can I handle a basic emergency without calling home?
- Do I make financial decisions or just follow what others suggest?

Self-reliance isn't about isolation. It's about being capable first, and generous later.

And it begins with one decision: "I will own the consequences of my money choices."

Once you do that, everything shifts.

The Emotional Shift No One Warns You About

Everyone talks about the thrill of earning. The pride of being paid. But few talk about the quieter feelings that show up alongside your first paycheck.

Guilt. Confusion. Pressure. Imposter syndrome. And a strange kind of loneliness.

You feel proud of earning, but unsure if you're doing it right.

You want to be responsible, but don't know where the line is.

You want to enjoy your money, but also fear losing control.

This is the emotional gray zone of early adulthood, and it shows up strongest in your financial life.

And yet, no one prepares you for this. Because until now, money wasn't your responsibility; it was someone else's concern.

Now, it's yours. Entirely. Quietly. Permanently.

Power Without Preparation: Why Earning Can Feel Unsettling

When you go from asking for money to having your own, it's not just liberating, it's destabilizing.

Because power without preparation leads to:

- Overspending in the name of "deserved" treats
- Avoiding budgets because they feel restrictive
- Using money to impress, not empower
- Carrying silent anxiety about "doing it wrong"

You're not alone if you feel this way.

Money changes how you see yourself. How others see you. And how you relate to the world around you.

This emotional upheaval is real. And if you don't address it, it can lead to:

- Unconscious rebellion ("It's my money, I'll do what I want.")
- Secret shame ("Everyone else seems to have it figured out.")
- Passive avoidance ("I'll deal with this later.")

You don't need more income to fix this. You need emotional clarity.

Redefining Financial Maturity

Here's what financial maturity really looks like in your early 20s:

- Not the size of your paycheck
- Not how many people you treat
- Not how expensive your gadgets are

But rather:

- How clearly you understand your income and expenses
- How responsibly you plan for your short-term and mid-term goals
- How honestly you acknowledge your current limits

Maturity doesn't mean restriction. It means making decisions from clarity, not confusion.

And clarity comes from three simple habits:

1. Reflecting: "Why am I spending on this?"
2. Recording: "Where is my money going?"
3. Recalibrating: "What do I need to change next month?"

These habits don't require apps or mentors. They require 15 minutes of attention per week.

The Power of the First Contribution

One of the most defining moments in a young person's financial life is not their first salary. It's their first conscious contribution to someone else.

Not out of obligation. Not for display. But from a place of pride.

It could be:

- Paying a part of your sibling's college tuition
- Sending money home during a tough month
- Gifting your mother something with your own money

These acts change something inside you.

They remind you that money isn't just a source of consumption. It's a tool of contribution.

And that transition, from user to giver, is what builds financial dignity.

Real Story: The Day Aarav Paid the Bill

Aarav, 22, landed his first campus placement in a tech firm. On his father's birthday, he took the family out to dinner at a quiet restaurant.

When the bill came, his father reached for the wallet. Aarav gently pushed his hand away and said, "I've got this."

The moment was small. But for Aarav, it was massive.

"That one gesture made me feel like I'd stepped into a new chapter. Not because I could afford a dinner, but because I'd earned the right to contribute."

The ability to give, when you weren't asked to, is the deepest proof of growth.

Ego vs. Gratitude: Two Roads from the Same Start Line

Early earnings can take you in two directions:

1. The Ego Path

- "I'm independent now. I don't need anyone."
- "If I'm earning, why should I take advice?"
- "This is my money; I don't have to explain."

This path often leads to isolation, poor decisions, and regret. Because arrogance builds distance, not growth.

2. The Gratitude Path

- "I'm thankful I can earn, now how do I grow wisely?"
- "Let me ask those ahead of me what they wish they knew at my age."
- "My success is possible because of others, I'll remember that."

This path leads to community, compounding wisdom, and peace of mind.

Gratitude isn't weakness. It's the strength to acknowledge that success is never solitary.

And that mindset will carry you further than any raise or bonus ever will.

Your Paycheck Isn't Just Money, It's a Mirror

Every rupee you earn is a reflection of:

- Your skills
- Your time
- Your discipline
- Your value in the current market

That doesn't mean your worth as a person is tied to your salary.

But your paycheck is a mirror of your current stage, and mirrors are powerful tools for growth if you're willing to look.

So instead of:

- Comparing your income to others
- Complaining about what it can't buy
- Craving shortcuts to "more"

Try this:

- Ask what skills you need to increase your income
- Explore how better money habits can stretch your rupee
- Reflect on what lifestyle truly brings you joy, not just stimulation

Your salary is not your ceiling. It's your starting point.

Celebrate, But Stay Conscious

Celebrating your first income is important. You've earned it. But celebration doesn't need to become justification.

"First salary" is not an excuse for reckless spending. It's a milestone, not a loophole.

So yes:

- Buy something small for yourself
- Take someone meaningful out
- Mark the moment proudly

But also:

- Pause and plan for the next 6 months
- Review your fixed and variable expenses
- Start thinking about your financial goals, not someone else's expectations

Because every celebration done with consciousness becomes a memory of pride, not a moment of regret.

From Earner to Decision-Maker: A Different Skillset

Earning money is one thing. Deciding what to do with it is another matter altogether.

Many young earners realize this too late. They assume that once income arrives, clarity will follow.

But money doesn't bring clarity. It exposes the absence of it.

Suddenly, you're faced with real questions:

- Do I buy that new phone or save for an emergency?
- Should I invest in a course or plan a trip?

- Is it okay to say no when a family member asks for financial help?

These aren't hypothetical. They're real-life choices, every month.

And to make them well, you need more than instinct. You need a decision-making framework.

The Three-Pillar Model for Financial Choices

Here's a simple model for navigating money decisions early in your earning years. Think of it as the three legs of a stable stool:

1. Logic: What do the numbers say?

- Can I afford this without going into debt?
- Does this expense align with my income, savings, and goals?

2. Emotion: How does this make me feel?

- Am I buying this out of pressure, boredom, insecurity, or genuine desire?
- Will I regret or respect this decision in a week?

3. Value: Does this align with who I want to be?

- Is this helping me grow, contribute, or sustain myself?
- Or is it just about fitting in or showing off?

A good financial decision is not one that ticks only one box. It's one that stands stable across all three.

Case Example: The Laptop Dilemma

Kritika, 24, was two months into her first job when her office laptop started lagging. She wanted to buy a personal laptop but wasn't sure which one.

Option 1: ₹90,000 MacBook

Option 2: ₹50,000 Windows laptop

Option 3: Continue with the office laptop for now

Her salary: ₹32,000/month. Savings so far: ₹8,000.

Let's apply the three-pillar model.

Logic: ₹90K is 3X her monthly salary and would require a loan. Not ideal.

Emotion: She loved the MacBook look, but knew she'd feel anxious with EMI stress.

Value: She needed performance, not prestige.

Option 2 aligned better with her current goals. She went with Option 2.

Three months later, she didn't regret it. She used the laptop to take freelance gigs and saved enough for travel.

That's what aligned decision-making looks like.

Four Ground Rules for Healthy Financial Conversations with Family

1. Be Transparent, Not Boastful

You don't need to share every rupee. But hiding your salary out of fear or guilt only breeds distance. Share basic figures honestly. Set the tone for openness.

2. Offer Before You're Asked

If you're in a position to help, do it proactively. Saying, "I'd like to take care of the monthly grocery bill now," earns respect. It shows maturity, not obligation.

3. Set Limits Gently, But Firmly

If a request feels out of reach, say: "I want to help, but I'll need time to plan for that." This keeps the dignity of both parties intact.

4. Don't Let Money Replace Communication

Sometimes, we give money because we're avoiding deeper talks about boundaries, resentment, and guilt. The real currency is emotional clarity, not cash.

Dealing with Guilt: The Invisible Drain

Many young earners carry an invisible burden: The guilt of having more options than their parents ever did.

They hesitate to spend on themselves.

They question every personal purchase.

They feel the need to justify their choices, even in their own head.

But here's what they forget: Your parents didn't struggle so that you would inherit their stress. They worked hard so you could have freedom, not anxiety.

And the best way to honor that is not through sacrifice. It's through responsibility.

Spend wisely. Give where you can. Build a life that reflects their values, not their hardships.

You're Not Selfish for Putting Yourself First (Sometimes)

Let's be clear: You are not selfish for:

- Saying "no" to unnecessary family expectations
- Choosing to save before gifting
- Investing in your own growth before giving it away

You're not neglecting others. You're preparing yourself to show up for them longer, better, stronger.

The airplane rule applies here: Put your oxygen mask on first, then assist others.

The Inner Tug-of-War: Spend, Save, or Support?

Every rupee in your account carries choices.

- One part wants to celebrate.
- Another wants to save.
- A third wants to give back.

The tension is real.

And that's where clarity becomes your compass. Clarity not built on fear, but on a vision of the life you want.

Here's a simple journaling question to answer every payday: "What kind of financial person do I want to become in the next 3 years?" "Does today's decision help me become that person?"

Not every choice will be perfect. But direction matters more than perfection.

The First Year Blueprint: What to Do With Your First Income Year

There's no perfect guidebook for the first year of earning, but there is a pattern among those who do it well.

They don't aim for perfection. They aim for progress. One decision at a time. One shift at a time.

Here's a practical blueprint that's worked for many first-jobbers across industries and income levels.

Month 1–2: Observe and Acknowledge

- Track every rupee. No budget yet. Just build awareness.
- Celebrate mindfully. One meaningful treat, not impulsive splurges.
- Talk to someone older and wiser. Learn what they wish they'd done differently.

This is the self-discovery phase. Don't rush decisions. Sit with your patterns.

Month 3–4: Create Systems

- Start a simple 50–30–20 budget and customize it based on your life.
- Set up auto-debits for basic savings; even ₹500/month is a start.
- Read one personal finance book or follow one trustworthy voice. Stick to it.

This is when earning starts to feel structured, not chaotic.

Month 5–6: Begin Contribution

- Start covering one consistent expense at home.
- Take responsibility for one shared cost with friends or flatmates.
- Buy something for someone else, with your heart, not your ego.

This is the transition from "earner" to "participant."

Month 7–9: Explore Growth

- Invest in a skill, course, or tool that increases your long-term income potential.
- Explore a side gig not for extra cash, but to stretch your ability.

- Learn about tax-saving instruments, EPF, and insurance. Don't wait till March.

Now you're building, not just spending.

Month 10–12: Reflect and Realign

- Revisit your original financial vision. Are you closer to it?
- Identify 2–3 bad money habits. Design strategies to correct them.
- Create a goal for Year 2, a purchase, a trip, or an amount saved.

This is when intention starts becoming identity.

From Receiving to Earning to Owning

This entire chapter is about a transformation.

From someone who waits for money to come to someone who makes it, manages it, and multiplies it over time.

The pocket money years taught you how to want. The paycheck years will teach you how to weigh.

What you spend on reflects what you prioritize. What you save for reflects what you believe in. What you give reflects who you are becoming.

Owning your financial life is not about becoming obsessed with money. It's about becoming conscious of your choices.

And that consciousness is what adulthood, real adulthood, is made of.

Rethinking Self-Reliance in the Indian Context

In many Western cultures, 18 is the age of financial independence.

In India, that number is blurry.

Some are financially independent at 21. Others are still asking parents for recharge money at 28. And neither is "wrong", but both need reflection.

Because true self-reliance isn't a number. It's a mindset.

It's asking:

- Do I rely on others out of necessity or convenience?
- Am I stretching myself or staying cushioned?
- Am I building capacity, or just buying time?

Self-reliance in India has its own rhythm. But if you don't step into it with intention, you might spend years postponing your own life.

Self-Reliance Is Not Isolation

Let's clear one last myth.

To be self-reliant does not mean severing ties with your parents, turning down any support, and playing the martyr.

That is not power; that is pride.

Financial Independence means having the confidence to support yourself, not being unsure of the choices you make, and to give because you desire to, not because you have to.

It is about saying: "I do not know it all. But I no longer need someone else to figure it out for me."

The Real Win: Quiet Confidence

The true marker of financial growth is not your salary. Not your savings. Not your investments.

It's the quiet confidence that says: I know where my money is going. I'm aware of what matters to me. I trust myself to make better decisions next month than I did last month.

It's not loud. It's not flashy. But it shows up in how you walk, speak, and plan.

And once that confidence kicks in, money stops being a mystery. It becomes a medium for expression, for contribution, for security, for peace.

Ritu's Responsibility

Ritu entered her first job with realistic expectations. She had already done part-time internships in college, so she knew the value of money. Her first step was to create a monthly budget. She understood her payslip, knew what PF meant, and set aside a small amount for savings immediately.

When friends asked for loans, she politely declined if it didn't fit her plan. She contributed a little at home without compromising her own stability. Over time, she built both self-reliance and confidence.

Ritu's story proves that independence doesn't come from just earning. It comes from managing what you earn wisely.

Contrasting Varun and Ritu: What was Different?

- Varun entered his first job with dreamy illusions, only to be crushed by deductions, debt, and the weight of others' expectations.
- Ritu entered with practical awareness, boundaries, and a plan, turning her paycheck into empowerment, not pressure.

Lesson: Earning money is only half the story. True independence comes from how you manage, protect, and respect it.

Ask Yourself: Do you want Varun's disappointment, or Ritu's responsibility?

Final Thoughts: This Is Just the Beginning

If you're reading this and feeling overwhelmed, take a breath.

You're not behind. You're just awake now.

That awareness puts you ahead of most.

Most people wait until a crisis to change their financial behavior. You're doing it with clarity. That is your edge.

You won't get it right all the time. You're not supposed to.

But if you reflect, course-correct, and stay conscious, you'll get better every single month.

That's all it takes.

Not perfection. Just direction.

Chapter 5: Fundamentals of Finance That Schools Must Teach

Aarav's Confusion

Aarav had just landed his first job. A promising role in a mid-sized IT company with a decent starting salary. He was excited, finally, money of his own. But within three months, he was already gasping for financial air.

Every payday felt like a festival: new sneakers, eating out at fancy cafes, UPI transfers to friends for impulsive plans, and, of course, the latest gadgets bought on EMI. He never checked his bank balance until it beeped with a low funds alert.

When he needed cash urgently, he turned to instant loan apps. One click, and the money would land in his account. He didn't think about the interest rates or repayment terms. After all, he thought, "I'll get my salary again next month."

But when repayment reminders began to pile up, along with credit card bills, Aarav panicked. He realised he couldn't explain half the transactions on his bank statement. He didn't understand why his salary always felt smaller than promised, and tax deductions seemed like a mystery theft. Insurance sounded boring, SIP was just an acronym people threw around, and inflation? He thought that only applied to vegetables in the market.

By the end of his first year of earning, Aarav wasn't celebrating his independence. He was trapped. The irony? He had worked hard to earn, but never learned how to manage. His story wasn't about lack of effort; it was about lack of fundamentals.

Why Schools Fail Us

If we think back to our school days, most of us spent years solving algebra equations or memorising chemical formulas, but almost no time learning how to budget money, what a bank statement really shows, or why insurance isn't optional.

We left school with degrees but no financial compass. So when life handed us our first paychecks, many stumbled just like Aarav, excited to earn, but clueless about how to protect, grow, and use that money wisely.

This chapter is about filling that gap. It's not theory, it's the toolbox we all should've received by age 18.

The Bedrock: Budgeting

The most underrated financial skill is also the simplest: budgeting.

A budget isn't a cage, it's a map. It tells you where your money goes and ensures it aligns with what actually matters to you.

Without it, you live Aarav's life: constantly wondering why the bank account feels empty when you've been "earning so much."

How to Start Budgeting

Step 1: Track Before You Plan. For one month, write down every rupee you spend. Don't judge, just observe.

Step 2: Divide Your Money. Use a simple rule: Needs (50%), Wants (30%), Savings/Investments (20%). Adjust based on your reality.

Step 3: Automate Savings. Treat savings like rent, non-negotiable. Transfer it out before you even see the balance.

Pro Tip: The "Envelope Method"

Even in a digital age, this method works. Create digital "envelopes" in your bank for groceries, bills, leisure, and savings. When one envelope empties, you stop spending.

Savings: The Safety Net

Money without savings is like walking a tightrope without a net. One slip, a medical emergency, a job delay, a sudden need, and you crash.

Saving doesn't mean hoarding. It means creating a cushion.

The Three Layers of Savings

1. **Emergency Fund:** 3–6 months of essential expenses kept in a liquid account.
2. **Short-Term Savings**: For things like trips, gadgets, or functions for the next 1–2 years.
3. **Long-Term Savings:** To fund goals like a home, further studies, a wedding or retirement.

The discipline of saving is not about denying yourself. It's about ensuring your future self has options. Aarav's panic in emergencies came because he had skipped this step.

Investing: Making Money Work for You

Saving alone isn't enough, especially in India, where inflation eats away quietly. That ₹1000 you leave idle today won't buy the same things five years later.

That's where investing comes in. It's not gambling. It's not a luxury for the rich. It's simply the science of making your money grow faster than inflation.

Basics Every Young Person Must Know

- **Inflation**: Prices rise every year. Your investments must outpace this.
- **SIP (Systematic Investment Plan):** A way to invest small, fixed amounts into mutual funds regularly. Simple, disciplined, powerful.
- **Diversification:** Never put all your money into one basket; spread it across equity, debt, and safer instruments.

The earlier you start, the more time your money has to compound. If Aarav had put even ₹2000/month into SIPs from his first salary, he'd be smiling at long-term growth instead of battling short-term debts.

Understanding Loans: Friend or Foe?

Loans aren't evil. They are tools. The problem begins when they're used recklessly.

A student loan for higher education? Useful.

A home loan within your means? Sensible.

A credit card swipe for a luxury watch you can't afford? Dangerous.

Golden Rules of Borrowing

1. Borrow for assets, not liabilities.
2. Keep your total EMI commitments below 30–35% of your income.
3. Understand the interest rate, not just the monthly amount.

Aarav's downfall wasn't that he borrowed. It was that he borrowed without understanding. He borrowed for consumption, not creation.

Demystifying the Jargon

One reason many youngsters stumble in their financial journey is that the language of money feels deliberately complicated. Banks, credit card companies, and even government websites are filled with terms that sound alien.

But finance isn't rocket science. It's just a different vocabulary. Once you learn it, you realise how simple it really is.

Let's strip down some essentials.

Inflation: The Silent Erosion

Think of inflation as a slow leak in your wallet.

Ten years ago, a plate of masala dosa cost ₹30. Today, in many cities, it's at least ₹70. That jump is not because the dosa got tastier, it's inflation.

If your savings don't grow faster than inflation, you're effectively getting poorer every year, even if the rupee amount looks the same.

Why it matters: If you save ₹1,00,000 in a simple account earning 3% interest while inflation is at 6%, you're losing purchasing power. The money grows in numbers but shrinks in value.

Insurance: Not Optional, Not Just for Old Age

Many young earners think insurance is unnecessary: "I'm healthy, why waste money?" That mindset is risky.

Insurance isn't about predicting disasters. It's about protecting against unpredictability.

- **Health Insurance**: Covers hospital bills, so a medical emergency doesn't wipe out your savings.
- **Term Life Insurance:** If you have dependents, this ensures they're secure if something happens to you.
- **General Insurance:** Covers assets like vehicles.

Why it matters: Aarav's mistake wasn't buying gadgets; it was not buying insurance. A single hospitalisation could undo months or years of effort.

SIP: The Discipline of Growth

SIP stands for Systematic Investment Plan. It's the most beginner-friendly way to start investing.

Instead of trying to time the market (which even experts fail at), you invest a fixed sum monthly into a mutual fund. Over the years, you buy at highs and lows, averaging out your cost.

Think of it as planting a tree. Each small deposit is a seed. With time and patience, it grows into a forest of wealth.

Even ₹2000/month invested from the age of 22 could potentially grow into lakhs by the time you're 30. The power lies not in the amount but in the consistency.

CIBIL Score: Your Financial Report Card

Imagine applying for a loan or a credit card and being rejected. Often, the reason is your CIBIL score.

CIBIL is India's credit bureau. It tracks how responsibly you've handled borrowed money.

- Pay EMIs on time? Score rises.
- Default or delay payments? Score falls.
- Never used credit? Score may be invisible.

Scores range from 300 to 900. Anything above 750 is considered strong.

Why it matters: Your CIBIL score affects whether you can buy a home, get a car loan, or even negotiate interest rates. Aarav's casual missed payments? They'll follow him for years.

Assets vs. Liabilities: The Real Difference

Schools taught us definitions. But in real life, the line is simpler:

- Assets put money in your pocket. (Stocks, rental property, mutual funds)
- Liabilities take money out. (Car loans, EMIs, gadgets bought on credit)

The confusion? Many people treat liabilities like assets. Aarav thought his new phone, bought on EMI, was an "investment." But unless it generates income, it's not.

How to Read a Payslip

For many, the first payslip is like decoding hieroglyphics. Acronyms everywhere: HRA, PF, TDS. But if you don't understand it, you don't understand your true income.

Key Components

- **Basic Salary:** The fixed component, often 30–40% of CTC.
- **HRA (House Rent Allowance):** Partially tax-exempt if you're paying rent.

- **PF (Provident Fund):** Forced savings that grow for retirement. Both you and your employer contribute.
- **TDS (Tax Deducted at Source):** Advance tax deducted from your salary.
- **CTC vs. Take-Home:** CTC includes everything the company spends on you. Take-home is what lands in your account. Big difference.

Aarav's shock at a smaller salary wasn't the company cheating him. It was ignorance about these terms.

How to Understand a Bank Statement

A bank statement is not just a list of debits and credits; it's a mirror of your habits.

What to Notice

- **Recurring charges:** Subscriptions you forgot.
- **Impulse spending patterns:** Late-night food orders, frequent UPI splurges.
- **Unfamiliar transactions:** Could signal fraud.
- **Balance trends:** Do you end each month higher, lower, or the same?

Reading your statement monthly helps you catch leaks early. It's like a doctor's check-up; ignore it, and problems grow silently.

Digital Payments and UPI Safety

UPI has transformed India. Sending ₹10 or ₹10,000 takes seconds. But convenience has a twin: risk.

Golden Rules of UPI Safety

- Never share your UPI PIN, even with "bank officials."
- Always double-check the receiver's name before confirming.
- Avoid scanning random QR codes.
- Don't click on payment links sent via SMS/WhatsApp.

Digital fraud is rising. But with awareness, UPI remains a powerful tool for smart, traceable transactions.

Basics of Income Tax

Taxes are unavoidable, but confusion is optional.

At the beginner level, remember:

- If you earn above the exemption limit (₹12 lakh annually, as outlined in the new tax regime), you pay tax.
- Slabs matter. Income is taxed progressively; higher income = higher slab.
- Investments in 80C (like PPF, ELSS, life insurance) reduce taxable income; however, if you choose the new tax regime, these deductions are not available.

Instead of panicking every March, plan from April. Tax is not theft; it's your contribution to the system. But ignorance costs money.

The Starter Toolkit for Every Young Earner

By now, you've seen how each concept connects. Here's a checklist you can build in your first year of earning:

1. A basic monthly budget (digital or notebook)
2. A savings account dedicated to emergencies
3. A health insurance policy (independent of your employer's)
4. A starter SIP in a mutual fund
5. A habit of checking your CIBIL score yearly
6. Understanding of your payslip and bank statement
7. Awareness of digital payment safety rules
8. Basic knowledge of your tax liability

This toolkit isn't fancy. But it's foundational. Without it, you're Aarav, earning, but lost. With it, you're equipped for growth.

From Concepts to Practice

It's one thing to know financial basics. It's another to weave them into daily life. Think of this as moving from reading a recipe to actually cooking a meal.

Knowledge alone won't stop you from repeating Aarav's mistakes. But the application will. Let's see how.

Designing a Practical Budget

Many people abandon budgeting because they overcomplicate it. They try fancy apps, spreadsheets, or unrealistic restrictions. A budget that's hard to maintain is like a diet that cuts out all food; you'll quit in frustration.

The key is simplicity.

The 50-30-20 Rule Reimagined

- 50% Needs: Rent, groceries, transport, bills
- 30% Wants: Eating out, hobbies, entertainment
- 20% Savings/Investments: Emergency fund, SIPs, insurance premiums

This isn't rigid math. Some months may tilt differently. What matters is balance. If your "wants" are consistently above 50%, you know why you're broke by the 20th.

Real-Life Example

Ritika earns ₹35,000/month. Shc allocates:

- ₹17,500 (Needs)
- ₹10,500 (Wants)
- ₹7,000 (Savings/Investments)

Within six months, she had ₹42,000 saved, not life-changing, but enough to cushion emergencies.

The lesson? Budgeting isn't punishment. It's permission to enjoy without guilt and to save without fear.

Setting Up an Emergency Fund

We've all heard of friends raising money overnight for medical crises or sudden job losses. Many times, the tragedy wasn't just the event; it was the lack of preparation.

A good emergency fund = 3 to 6 months of expenses.

How to Build It Slowly

- Start with one month's expenses in a separate savings account.
- Add to it every month, even if it's just ₹1000 to it.
- Keep it liquid, don't invest it in long-term funds.

Think of it as paying rent to your future self. You may never use it, but the peace of mind itself is priceless.

Insurance in Real Life

Theory: "Buy insurance."

Reality: "Which policy? Which company? How much cover?"

Health Insurance

- Opt for at least ₹5–10 lakh cover in metros (hospital costs soar fast).
- Don't rely solely on employer insurance; it lapses when you leave.

- Read inclusions and exclusions carefully (pre-existing illnesses, room rent caps).

Life Insurance

- Term insurance is the only product worth considering at a young age.
- If you don't have dependents, skip it for now.
- Ignore policies mixing insurance + investment. They're expensive and inefficient.

Vehicle Insurance

- Always opt for comprehensive, not just third-party liability. That "savings" today can cost lakhs later.

Insurance isn't sexy. But neither is bankruptcy.

Getting Started with SIPs

For beginners, SIPs can feel intimidating, mutual funds, NAVs, and markets. But you don't need to master every detail to begin.

How to Start

- Open an account with a trusted fund house or via your bank.
- Pick a large-cap index fund to begin; it's safer and easier.
- Start with as little as ₹500/month. Increase as income grows.

Why Start Early

If you invest ₹3000/month from age 22 at an average 12% return:

- By age 32 → ~₹7.5 lakh
- By age 42 → ~₹25 lakh
- By age 52 → ~₹80 lakh

That's the magic of compounding, often called the eighth wonder of the world.

But what if you start late? If you begin the same ₹3000/month at age 32 (just 10 years later):

- By age 42 → ~₹7.5 lakh (what the early starter had at 32)
- By age 52 → ~₹25 lakh (what the early starter had at 42)

In other words, starting 10 years late pushes you an entire decade behind in wealth creation; you can't "catch up" without investing much more each month.

Age	Early Starter (begins at 22)	Late Starter (begins at 32)
32	~₹7.5 lakh	₹0
42	~₹25 lakh	~₹7.5 lakh

52	~₹80 lakh	~₹25 lakh

The early starter is always one full decade ahead.

To match the early starter, a late starter would need to invest 3x more per month (around ₹9000) after age 32.

Aarav didn't know this. He believed investments were for later, for "settled" people. But in truth, investing is what helps you settle faster.

Tracking CIBIL in Practice

Checking your CIBIL score once a year should be as routine as a health check-up.

Practical Tips

- Use free portals or CIBIL's own website.
- If your score is below 700, avoid new loans until it improves.
- Pay credit card bills in full, not just minimum dues.
- Don't apply for multiple loans simultaneously (each rejection hurts your score).

CIBIL isn't about impressing banks. It's about proving to yourself that you're reliable with money.

Reading a Payslip in Context

Let's decode a sample scenario:

Rohan's first payslip shows:

- Basic: ₹20,000
- HRA: ₹8,000
- Other Allowances: ₹7,000
- Employer PF Contribution: ₹2,400
- Deductions (TDS + Employee PF): ₹4,800
- Take-home: ~₹30,200

Rohan thought he "earned" ₹37,000. But CTC included employer PF, which doesn't land in his bank. Once he understood this, he planned his expenses on his actual take-home, not the illusion of CTC.

This simple clarity prevents frustration.

Reading a Bank Statement with Awareness

If you review your statement monthly, ask:

- Do I see repeated food delivery transactions?
- Any unused subscriptions draining ₹200–500 each?
- Am I paying penalties for late bill payments?
- Does my balance steadily rise, fall, or remain flat?

Aarav ignored these patterns. Ritika didn't. By cancelling 3 unused subscriptions, she saved ₹1500/month, ₹18,000 a year. Small leaks sink big ships.

UPI Safety in Daily Use

Fraudsters thrive on carelessness, not intelligence. Even smart youngsters fall for scams because they're rushed.

Real-Life Case

Sneha received a UPI link saying she'd won cashback. She clicked, entered her PIN, and lost ₹15,000.

Lesson: Banks will never ask for PINs via links. If something feels urgent, it's usually fake.

Everyday Habits

- Verify merchant names before paying.
- Don't store PINs in your phone's notes app.
- Enable transaction SMS alerts to catch fraud instantly.

Income Tax: The Beginner's Checklist

Filing taxes seems daunting, but here's a simple checklist:

- Register on the income tax portal early.
- Collect Form 16 (from your employer).
- Check if the old or the new regime is appropriate for you by consulting a CA.
- Use Section 80C instruments (PF, ELSS, insurance) to reduce liability.
- File before the deadline, penalties add up.

Youngsters often avoid taxes out of fear. But knowledge turns fear into clarity.

A Day in the Life of Smart Finance

To tie this together, let's imagine how a financially aware youngster lives:

- **Morning:** Checks monthly budget app while sipping chai.
- **Afternoon**: Gets a notification of mutual fund SIP debit, smiles instead of worrying.
- **Evening:** Reviews bank statement, cancels unused gym membership.
- **Weekend:** Sets aside time to file tax-saving documents.

It's not about obsession. It's about rhythm, small, consistent actions that prevent big mistakes.

From Basics to Confidence

Knowing financial concepts is useful. Practising them is powerful. But the real transformation happens when these practices shift how you feel about money.

Most young earners live with low-level financial anxiety:

- Will my salary last the month?
- Am I paying too much tax?
- What if an emergency hits?

- Am I falling behind my peers?

Confidence doesn't come from earning more. It comes from clarity. When you understand your payslip, your bank statement, your SIPs, and your insurance, you stop fearing the unknown. Money becomes a partner, not a puzzle.

Why Fundamentals Matter More Than Fancy Tricks

It's tempting to skip the basics and jump into trading stocks, crypto, or speculative bets. But skipping steps is like trying to run before you can walk.

Ask anyone who lost lakhs in day trading; they didn't lose because they were unlucky. They lost because they never mastered budgeting, saving, and disciplined investing first.

Aarav's story isn't extreme. It's common. And his downfall wasn't poor income, it was ignoring fundamentals.

The Psychological Edge

Practising financial basics doesn't just help your wallet. It helps your mind.

1. **Control:** When you know where your money goes, you feel in charge of your life.
2. **Peace:** Emergency funds reduce the background worry of "what if something happens?"
3. **Freedom:** Savings and investments mean you can say no to toxic jobs or unhealthy financial dependence.

4. **Confidence:** Reading payslips and bank statements fluently removes the intimidation of "financial language."

Money stress is one of the biggest causes of anxiety in young adults. Mastering fundamentals doesn't erase challenges, but it arms you with calm responses instead of panicked reactions.

How Fundamentals Compound Over Time

The beauty of these basics is that they don't just help now, they build a foundation for decades.

- A ₹2000 SIP started at 23 isn't impressive by 24, but by 33, it's worth lakhs.
- Reading your bank statement monthly might save only ₹500–1000 a month in leaks. Over 5 years, that's ₹60,000 saved and redirected.
- Filing taxes properly avoids penalties and builds a record that helps when applying for loans or visas.

Each small action compounds, not just financially but emotionally. You evolve from being "someone who spends and hopes" to "someone who plans and acts."

Building Discipline Without Feeling Restricted

The biggest myth about personal finance is that it's about sacrifice. People fear that budgeting means giving up fun, that saving means missing out.

In truth, discipline creates more space for enjoyment.

Imagine two friends:

- Riya spends freely, never budgets. She enjoys weekends but panics by the 20th of each month.
- Kavya budgets, saves, and invests. She too enjoys weekends, but with no guilt. She books trips months in advance because she has planned for them.

Who's freer? The one with discipline.

The Indian Context: Why Fundamentals Are Even More Crucial

In India, youngsters face unique challenges:

- Families often expect financial contribution.
- Peer pressure to "show" success through brands is intense.
- Digital payment ease makes overspending effortless.
- Schools rarely cover financial basics.

This means you don't just need financial literacy; you need it urgently. Fundamentals aren't "good to know." They're survival skills in today's India.

Everyday Scenarios Where Basics Save You

Let's walk through common situations where fundamentals make the difference:

Unexpected Medical Expense

Without insurance, you drain savings, borrow money, or take high-interest loans.

With insurance, the policy absorbs most of the shock.

First Loan Application

With poor CIBIL, you face rejection, higher interest rates, and financial stress.

With a strong CIBIL, you get smooth approval, lower EMIs, and peace of mind.

Paycheck Confusion

Without understanding payslips, there's constant frustration about "low salary."

With clarity, there's realistic planning, reduced stress.

Peer Pressure Weekend

Without budgeting, you end up splurging ₹5000 and regret it later.

With budgeting, you enjoy within your "wants" allocation, with no guilt.

These everyday wins don't look dramatic. But they prevent the slow financial bleed that destroys stability over time.

Making Finance a Life Skill

Think about how we treat driving. We don't say, "I'm not a car person, I won't learn." Because driving is a life skill.

Finance deserves the same treatment. You don't have to be an "investment geek" to learn the basics. You just need enough to drive your financial life safely.

Schools may not have taught us. But that doesn't mean we can't learn now and pass it on to the next generation.

From Aarav to Awareness

By now, you can see Aarav's mistakes differently. They weren't moral failings. There were gaps in knowledge.

- If he had learned budgeting, he wouldn't have panicked at low balances.
- If he had insurance, he wouldn't fear emergencies.
- If he had SIPs, he'd be excited about growth, not trapped in debt.
- If he had checked his CIBIL, he wouldn't have been rejected for loans.

One by one, the fundamentals could have saved him.

Bridging the "School Gap"

This chapter isn't just a guide. It's a manifesto for what schools should have taught us:

- How to earn, save, and invest.

- How to borrow wisely.
- How to read payslips and statements.
- How to protect ourselves with insurance.
- How to stay safe in a digital money world.

If we start teaching these basics in households, colleges, and workplaces, the next generation won't face the same struggles.

The Confidence Loop

Once you practice fundamentals, something magical happens:

- Clarity reduces stress.
- Reduced stress leads to better decisions.
- Better decisions grow your money.
- Growth gives you more confidence.
- Confidence reinforces clarity.

It becomes a loop, a self-sustaining cycle of financial empowerment.

That's the opposite of Aarav's loop: confusion → mistakes → stress → more mistakes.

Rithika's Clarity

Rithika, unlike Aarav, didn't step into the professional world blindly. Her upbringing hadn't included formal financial education either; her school never taught her what "inflation" meant, or why insurance was important. But she had curiosity, and she believed that money deserved as much attention as her career or health.

When she received her first internship stipend of ₹8,000, she resisted the urge to spend it all on shopping. Instead, she opened a savings account separate from her spending account. It felt small, but to her, it was symbolic: "I'll start building my future with this."

By the time she joined her first job, she already understood the 50-30-20 budget. She allocated part of her income to needs, a portion to wants, and a strict slice to savings. While friends laughed at her "boring discipline," she was never the one scrambling for money by mid-month.

The Toolkit in Action

Rithika's story is powerful not because she earned more, but because she applied the fundamentals.

- **Budgeting:** She tracked every rupee, but without obsessing. For her, it wasn't about cutting fun; it was about knowing where her money went.
- **Savings:** She built an emergency fund worth 4 months' expenses within her first year. That fund sat quietly in a liquid account, untouched but ready.
- **Insurance:** Rithika didn't wait for an emergency. She bought independent health insurance early, ensuring she wasn't tied only to her employer's plan.

- **Investing:** She started a small SIP, ₹1500 a month. Over the years, she increased it steadily. By her late twenties, compounding had already begun rewarding her discipline.
- **CIBIL Awareness:** She never defaulted on payments. Her score crossed 780, allowing her to negotiate a lower interest rate when she eventually took a car loan.
- **Payslip Clarity:** Rithika knew the difference between CTC and take-home. She planned expenses realistically. Taxes weren't a surprise; they were a line item in her monthly plan.
- **Digital Safety:** She double-checked every UPI transfer, never clicked suspicious links, and kept her bank apps secure.

The Results

By the age of 28, Rithika was earning a respectable salary. But more importantly, she had:

- Zero debt beyond planned EMIs.
- A growing investment portfolio.
- Health and vehicle insurance in place.
- A CIBIL score that made banks eager to lend.
- The confidence to plan for bigger goals like higher education abroad.

When her peers worried about job instability, she didn't panic. Her emergency fund and savings gave her options.

When a friend fell into debt due to reckless BNPL usage, she offered empathy but also quiet proof that discipline works better than denial.

Rithika vs. Aarav: Two Paths

Both Aarav and Rithika began at the same starting line: educated, ambitious, eager to earn. But their financial journeys diverged dramatically.

- Aarav ignored the fundamentals. Result: confusion, debt, stress.
- Rithika practised the fundamentals. Result: clarity, growth, confidence.

The difference wasn't income. It wasn't luck. It was financial literacy applied early.

Why You Can Be Rithika Too

It's easy to think, "I'll start later, once I earn more." But Rithika didn't wait for a high salary. She began with ₹1500 SIPs and ₹500 monthly savings. She knew discipline mattered more than amount.

The truth is: anyone can follow this path. You don't need extraordinary intelligence. You don't need rich parents. You don't need to sacrifice joy.

You just need to build your personal finance toolkit:

- Budget monthly
- Build an emergency fund
- Buy insurance wisely
- Start SIPs early
- Protect your CIBIL score
- Read your payslip and bank statement
- Stay safe with digital payments
- Plan for taxes proactively

This toolkit is your armour. It's what schools should've handed you. Since they didn't, this book is doing it now.

Aarav or Rithika?

Imagine standing at a crossroads. On one path lies Aarav's world: shiny purchases, careless borrowing, and hidden traps that lead to long-term stress. On the other path lies Rithika's world: clarity, protection, steady growth, and freedom to live without fear.

The choice is yours.

Every rupee you earn is a seed. Waste it, and it disappears. Plant it with care, and it grows into shade for tomorrow. Aarav let his seeds scatter in the wind. Rithika planted hers wisely.

From today onwards, ask yourself: Who do I want to be, Aarav or Rithika?

If you've read this far, you already know the answer.

Chapter 6: Breaking the Mindsets - Earning, Spending, and Talking Money

Raghav's Reality

Raghav had grown up in a conventional family in Lucknow. His parents adored him, but they also bore inherited beliefs. For his parents, academics were paramount. Money matter was either pushed under the carpet or spoken in hushed tones after the children were asleep.

"Focus on studies, not on earning," his father often said whenever Raghav showed interest in doing small gigs during college. His mother added, "Money talk spoils kids. You'll learn when the time comes."

So Raghav never questioned these ideas.

When his peers began doing internships during college, he called them desperate. "Why earn ₹5,000 when you can study?" he thought. He was proud to be "shielded" by his parents. His father paid for all his bills, be it mobile bills or buying clothes online.

Even when Raghav landed his first job at 24, the trend followed. He had no idea what financial independence felt like. His salary went through his fingers since he never knew how to budget. He spent it on gadgets and outings, believing that's what success was.

Talking about money with his parents? Unthinkable. They still believed it was rude to ask questions like "How much do we spend on groceries?" or "What's our monthly household income?"

By the age of 30, reality struck. His father retired without a clear plan for finances, and overnight, the family was looking up to Raghav to take on responsibilities he was ill-equipped for. He didn't even know how to handle his salary, much less support others. He panicked, attributing it to his job, to the economy, everyone except the real culprit: a mindset that eschewed discussions about money and derailed early financial responsibility.

Raghav's is not an unusual story. It's the tale of thousands of young Indians who are brought up in households where money is either never discussed or is equated with greed. This silence conditions us to hold attitudes that harm us later in life.

This chapter is about coming down those barriers, altered modes of thinking, speaking, and behaving around money.

Cultural Resistance to Early Earning

In most Indian households, there's an unwritten rule: "Students are not supposed to work; they should only focus on studies."

The intention is pure; parents don't want children to be distracted from studying, but the consequence is alarming. It postpones financial wisdom and autonomy. Young adults enter the workforce with no experience in the real world. They handle their first paycheck like a lottery ticket, not an obligation. They experiment with budgeting through humiliating errors rather than cautionary experiments.

Compare this with nations where teens have part-time jobs, not because families are economically poor, but because it instills a work ethic and money sense at an early age.

Working while studying in college isn't greed or a distraction. It's a learning value. Even a ₹3,000 freelance project teaches lessons no school can: time management, negotiation, saving culture, and respect for hard-earned money.

Don't buy into the myth that earning early ruins academics; it doesn't. In fact, earning while studying can make you sharper and more responsible.

The Stigma Around Talking About Money

"Don't talk about money around kids."

"Don't question income, it's disrespectful."

Ring a bell? These lines of advice have spawned generations of adults who are uneasy talking about salary, costs, or investments with their loved ones.

Why is it bad? Children learn that money is a secret, not an art. Partners shy away from open conversation regarding money, and there's trouble down the road. Teenagers make blind choices because they have never witnessed open planning.

Contrast this with families that normalise money conversations. When children see parents budgeting, discussing insurance, or planning investments, they absorb financial discipline naturally.

Healthy Money Talk From Parents Looks Like:

- Sharing why they're saving for an emergency fund.
- Explaining monthly expenses without making their kids feel burdened.
- Teaching the kids the difference between needs and wants through real examples.

If your parents do this, they know, "Money talk is not corruption; it's education."

Breaking Gender Stereotypes in Financial Roles

In most households, men remain the "providers," and women are "spenders" or "homemakers." Even well-educated families are not immune to this fallacy.

The problem? Women receive very little exposure to handling money, making them weak in a crisis. Men feel obliged to carry the financial burden themselves, leading to stress and resentment.

This stereotype is not only unjust, it's risky. Life is full of surprises. Sickness, losing one's job, or losing a partner can strike anyone. Financial literacy must never be gender-based.

How to Break It?

- Learn the basics of banking, budgeting, and investing, regardless of gender.
- Don't assume money management is someone else's job. If you're in a relationship, talk about financial goals openly.

- Build equality in money matters early, share responsibility, share decisions, share knowledge.

Real empowerment starts with you knowing your numbers. The more financially aware you are, the stronger your future becomes.

How Parental Cushioning Stunts Financial Development

Numerous Indian parents overspend themselves to protect their children from hardship. They cover all expenses, education, devices, even car or housing down payments. Though that is done out of love, it tends to breed dependency.

What Then? Young adults put off financial autonomy. They assume money comes automatically, with parents "bailing them out." They don't plan because "Papa will take care of it."

Short-term, it's reassuring. Long-term, it's devastating. Life won't let anyone off the hook when it comes to money, and the sooner you deal with it, the more manageable it is.

What can you do? Start managing your allowance or pocket money like a budget. If you want something extra, explore part-time work or gigs instead of depending on handouts. Be real about family finances; don't assume money is unlimited. And stop waiting for someone else to teach you; move from being sheltered to being prepared.

Fostering Financial Discourse Between Parents and Children

Picture a dinner with the family where, rather than discussing only movies or politics, parents and children are discussing savings aims, investments, or how to keep within a vacation budget.

Sounds odd? It shouldn't be.

Financial discussions do teach decision-making skills, the importance of planning, and the reality of expenses and trade-offs.

If your parents don't have these discussions with you, perhaps you can begin initiating such discussions with them, because they will serve a great lesson in you realising that money is never unlimited.

Redefining Success in Terms of Anything but Luxury and Status Symbols

Our culture idolises conspicuous wealth, luxury clothes, flashy vehicles, and destination weddings. Social media exacerbates.

But success is not about what you parade. It's about what you maintain.

Having a luxury vehicle on EMIs you can't even begin to afford isn't success; it's a debt trap.

Taking a loan for a vacation isn't freedom; it's financial slavery disguised as lifestyle.

The real flex?

Being debt-free. Having an emergency fund. Investing consistently. Sleeping peacefully without worrying about credit card bills.

Change the definition of success in your mind, and you'll change your financial future.

How to Break the Silence Around Money

Most money issues aren't the result of numbers; they are the result of silence. Silence regarding income, expenditures, savings, and even debt. Shattering this silence doesn't involve posting your pay on Facebook; it involves creating healthy, open discussions at home.

Start Small

Don't feel like you need to master everything about finance overnight. Start with the basics:

- Understand why budgeting matters in daily life.
- Look at common expenses like electricity or internet bills and see how small changes save money.
- Try planning a trip or hangout with friends on a fixed budget.

These simple steps make money management feel natural, not intimidating.

Making Money Talk A Normal Part of Life

Instead of waiting for someone else to bring up money, start asking yourself questions like: "If I had ₹5000 coming in next month, how would I use it?"

Think about:

- What's a real need vs. just a want?
- How would you plan your spending so nothing is wasted?
- How much could you save?

Take it further. Get involved in real decisions: compare mobile plans, check subscription costs, or even help plan a budget for a big purchase at home.

The more you make money talk a normal part of life now, the easier it'll be to manage it confidently later.

Fostering Early Income Without Guilt

One of the most harmful myths is: "If you earn early, you're diverted from studies."

In real life, freelancing, part-time jobs, or internships give a lesson in time management and grit. They also teach the importance of hard work.

Here are some action steps for you to take in this regard:

- Steer clear of exploitative or study-eating jobs.
- Prioritise education over earnings in the first place.

- Utilise earnings to develop habits, open a savings account, create a very small SIP, or volunteer contributions towards household expenses.

Early earning develops confidence, not arrogance. It teaches humility, responsibility, and self-reliance, values schools can't impart.

Shattering Gender Stereotypes in Financial Careers

Indian families tend to perpetuate stereotypes inadvertently. Comments such as:

"Beta will earn money for us."

"Girls don't need to worry about money; their husbands will take care of it."

These notions may sound innocent, but they have actual ramifications. Women become financially dependent, and men absorb unhealthy pressure.

How to Change It

- **Equal Exposure:** Learn the basics: opening a bank account, paying bills, and investing, regardless of gender.
- **Shared Responsibility:** If you're part of a household or relationship, share money decisions instead of leaving it to someone else.
- **Celebrate Competence:** Being financially smart isn't about gender. It's about confidence and independence.

Disrupting this stereotype isn't only empowering women, it de-stresses men.

Reducing Over-Cushioning by Parents

Indian parents commonly view financial hardship as something to be avoided at all costs. Although protection is normal, over-protection creates dependency.

Healthy Cushioning vs Over-Cushioning

Healthy: Providing for education and necessities, but teaching self-reliance in later years.

Over: Providing for every luxury, paying credit card bills, or financing luxuries.

You need to stop depending on this financial cushioning.

To break the habit:

- Treat your allowance like a fixed budget; don't expect bailouts for overspending.
- Want a new gadget? Save up or try a part-time gig instead of relying on someone else.
- Practice delayed gratification - good things take time, and that's okay.

Learning this now will prepare you for the real world, where independence matters most.

Redefining Success in a Hyper-Consumer World

Instagram and influencers have redefined "cool" as pricey vacations, designer labels, and high-end gadgets. Kids feel they must keep up, even to the point of debt.

But actual success isn't what appears good on a headline; it's what feels good in real life.

Practical Redefinition

Success = Holding assets, not liabilities.

Success = Inner peace, not constant EMIs.

Success = Freedom to refuse a toxic job, because you have savings.

Don't link your self-worth to expensive weddings, gifts, or what people think on social media. Real flex? Financial freedom, not financial show-off.

The new success mantra needs to be: Freedom > Flexing, Security > Status.

How to Start Financial Conversations Without Awkwardness

Families tend to steer clear of money conversations due to fear of fights or judgment. Here's how to turn it positive:

Choose the Right Time

Steer clear of stressful moments, such as after a major loss or after a fight. Opt for peaceful environments.

Frame It in a Positive Way

Rather than saying, "We spend too much," say, "How can we save together?"

Engage Everyone

Financial literacy is for everyone: children, teenagers, and adults. Let everyone contribute ideas.

Keep It Solution-Focused

The objective isn't fault; it's preparation. Concentrate on what you can do today, not yesterday's errors.

The Long-Term Payoff of Shattering These Mindsets

When families make money matters and shared responsibility a normal part of life:

- Kids become self-assured, not ignorant.
- Women become independent and secure.
- Men are not solely responsible, losing less sleep.

Parents help children grow into financially responsible adults rather than entitled dependents. This is how we turn cultural obstacles into cultural assets.

Shattering the "Don't Ask, Don't Tell" Money Culture

For years, Indian families treated money like a dirty secret. It was taboo to ask about salary even among family members. The consequence? Adults joined the workforce in ignorance regarding taxes, saving, or taking loans.

How to Fix This

Normalise the following questions: "What's the difference between CTC and take-home?" or "How much should I save from my first salary?"

Avoid shaming: If one does confess financial ignorance, advise them rather than jeer.

Create openness: Transparency creates trust and confidence.

Role Models Within Families

You pick up money habits more from what you see than what you hear. If the people around you keep flaunting luxury cars or big weddings on credit, the unspoken message is: "Looking rich matters more than being stable."

Flip that mindset for yourself:

- Get excited about an investment growing, not just buying the latest gadget.
- Celebrate being debt-free as much as you would buying something new.
- Feel proud when you skip an unnecessary upgrade because you're saving for something bigger and better.

How to Cope with Peer and Social Pressure

Even financially conscious teens have a weak moment when friends show off. Here's how to cope:

- **Keep reminding yourself:** Social media = highlight reel, not real life.

- **Compare goals, not tools:** Are you creating security or seeking validation?
- **Practice delayed gratification:** If you still need that gadget in 30 days, get it, but with budgeted funds, not debt.

Introducing Money Conversations in Schools

Although the chapter addresses families, schools have a big impact as well. Consider if every school had:

- Simple budgeting practice in math class.
- Group conversations about saving and spending behaviour.
- Workshops about digital protection and financial fraud.

It's time we urged systemic change as well. But till then, families can step in.

Why This Mindset Shift Matters More Than Ever

India is experiencing a financial revolution:

- UPI and digital payments are ubiquitous.
- Credit access has never been simpler.
- Social media raises consumption pressure.

Unless mindsets shift, this convenience will convert into chaos, debt traps, scams, and financial stress.

Shattering these old-time beliefs isn't merely forward thinking. It's survival.

The Psychology of Money Mindsets

Money is not just numbers; it's a feeling. Each and every money belief we have influences how we work, spend, save, and discuss money.

If you were a kid watching "Money talk is impolite," you'd be filled with guilt while watching yourself request a raise.

If you were taught "Men manage money," you may dismiss financial education as a woman or feel bogged down as a man.

If your parents protected you from financial difficulties, you will anticipate that life will do the same for you.

Mindset change isn't merely about enhancing money; it's about changing emotional habits.

The Stress Cycle of Silence

When families don't talk about money, they inadvertently create tension down the line:

- Parents feel alone handling everything themselves.
- Children grow up uninformed and make expensive errors.
- Couples argue because expectations were never communicated.

This silence perpetuates a cycle: Ignorance → Mismanagement → Stress → More Silence.

Breaking it turns the cycle into: Awareness → Planning → Confidence → Open Conversations.

Why Openness Decreases Anxiety

Financial fear is widespread among young Indians today:

"Am I saving enough?"

"What if I lose my job?"

"Will I ever afford a house?"

Most of this fear arises out of uncertainty. And uncertainty flourishes in silence.

Discussing money openly, at home or in relationships, brings clarity. Clarity decreases fear. Fear replaced by planning brings peace.

Why Gender-Neutral Finance Makes Relationships Stronger

When someone takes all the finances, two dangers arise:

1. Overload for one partner.
2. Ignorance for the other.

Both lead to dependency. Dependency leads to imbalance. Imbalance leads to resentment.

But when both partners share responsibility, budgeting, investing, and decision-making, three things happen:

1. **Transparency:** No secrets, no surprises.
2. **Security:** Either can handle finances in emergencies.
3. **Respect:** Financial knowledge fosters equality, not power plays.

Shattering gender stereotypes isn't just social progress; it's relationship insurance.

The Confidence That Comes from Early Earning

Earning early, even modestly, has a psychological effect that textbooks can't offer.

You earn respect for money because you earned it. You feel independent, not entitled. You develop identity through contribution, not consumption.

Compare this to the folks who earn late and blow money because they never learned restraint. The sooner you manage money, the sooner you learn control.

The Hidden Damage of Over-Cushioning

When parents overprotect children financially, they inadvertently cause:

Low resilience: Children freak out at their initial financial crisis.

Entitlement: "If I fall, someone will catch me."

Delayed independence: They remain dependent on parents well beyond a reasonable age.

Breaking this cycle isn't about severity; it's about preparation. Guided exposure to financial responsibility develops problem-solving abilities.

Redefining Success = Redefining Mental Peace

The world tells us success equals "looking rich." Social media compounds the issue. But pursuing this mirage causes debt and anxiety.

When you shatter this mindset and consider success to be freedom, security, and peace, your decisions change.

You choose experiences over bragging.

You say "no" to debt for status.

You prioritise progress over comparison.

And here's the reality: true confidence isn't in the car that you drive, it's in knowing that you own it debt-free.

How Families Benefit from Financial Transparency

When families open up about money:

- Kids gain practical skills early on.
- Parents minimise future reliance.
- Couples prevent conflicts over hidden spending or unrealistic expectations.

Transparency builds trust, and trust builds strength, financial and emotional.

Simple Daily Habits to Reinforce New Mindsets

Big changes start small. Try these:

- Once a week, share a financial tip with family over dinner.

- As a teenager, take responsibility for one household expense (like the electricity bill).
- Every month, review spending as a family without blame, and focus on learning.
- For couples, schedule a "money date" every month to talk about goals and budgets.

These practices routine money conversations and erode old taboos over time.

From Shame to Strategy

The earlier money mystique culture was rooted in fear: fear of judgment, fear of greed, fear of loss. But that fear is now turned into financial illiteracy.

Shattering these attitudes isn't about flaunting riches; it's about creating security and self-assurance. It's about trading shame for strategy, secrecy for strength.

Ananya's Way

Ananya was born in Pune, in a middle-class family that valued openness and shared responsibility. Her parents were not rich, but they were smart.

Unlike Raghav's home, where money was a taboo subject, Ananya's family made money a part of everyday conversation, not in a stressful way, but as a learning tool.

When she was 14, her father explained why they were delaying the purchase of a new car, “We’re saving for your education, Ananya. A car can wait, but your future can’t.”

That one conversation, though, taught her something most teens never learn: money choices are about prioritising, not deprivation.

Ananya's parents never said, "You just study, don't worry about money." In fact, they urged her to do summer internships, not only for the money, but for the learning.

When she made ₹6,000 in her first internship, her mom didn't tell her to "Save it all." Rather, she told her, "Use some for yourself, but save at least 30%. That is how you learn balance."

This counsel influenced Ananya's thinking. She didn't perceive earning as greed; she perceived earning as autonomy.

In Ananya's household, money management wasn't a matter of gender. Her brother and she both learned to pay bills, balance bank accounts, and even shop for insurance.

This experience bred confidence. She knew she was capable of taking care of her own finances, not waiting for husband or father to "take care of everything."

When her college friends boasted about shopping for costly gadgets on EMI, Ananya smiled but did not join the race. She wondered: "Do I want to appear rich now, or remain free in the future?"

Her response was definitive. She had put her stipend into a small SIP rather than blowing it on the newest phone. When friends upgraded their phones annually, she kept hers for four years, but her SIP by then had accumulated enough to invest in an international certification course.

Ananya got her first job at 23. She didn't accelerate her lifestyle upgrade because her parents had prepared her for this stage.

She went over her payslip with her father, not to brag, but to learn about deductions and tax planning.

She initiated a health insurance policy separate from her company plan.

She was responsible with her expenses and focused on creating an emergency fund.

Her peers ridiculed her "boring" method initially, but three years down the line, when the industry experienced layoffs, Ananya was not fazed. She had six months' worth of spending money in the bank and did not owe anyone anything.

Why Ananya Succeeded?

The difference was not luck. It was attitude.

Openness: Her family taught her to make money normal.

Early Earning: Internships trained her to appreciate money.

Equality: She never thought about finances as "someone else's responsibility."

Redefined Success: She preferred freedom over showing off.

Today, Ananya is not a millionaire, but she's financially independent. She has a secure investment portfolio, no debt, and faith that she'll be able to survive any tempest life unleashes upon her.

Raghav vs. Ananya: Two Mindsets, Two Futures

Raghav and Ananya were both smart, educated, and driven. Both cared about their families. But their paths took different turns due to their mindsets.

1. Raghav's family never discussed money → He walked into adulthood ill-prepared.
2. Ananya's family normalised money conversations → She entered adulthood empowered.

One struggled to adjust; the other thrived.

Your Takeaway

If you've grown up with silence, stereotypes, or cushioning, don't blame yourself or your parents. They acted with love, but now it's your turn to choose better.

Talk about money with your family.

Encourage equal responsibility regardless of gender.

Start earning early, not for luxury, but for learning.

Redefine success as freedom, not status.

Mindsets are passed down, but they can also be transformed. Begin with one conversation today. Shatter the silence. Forge the strength.

Money isn't only numbers; it's culture, routines, and assumptions. We've had it wrong for too long, assuming it was a secret or a sign. Now it's time to make it a skill.

Raghav's tale is a warning. Ananya's tale is an invitation.

Which way will you go?

The age-old way of silence and stereotypes, or the new way of openness and independence?

The decision will determine not only your bank balance, but your confidence, relationships, and a good night's sleep.

The transformation starts with attitude. Attitude starts with you.

Chapter 7: The Digital Money Maze – Staying Smart in a Cashless World

Aarav's Swipes and Slips

Aarav, a 22-year-old college student in Bengaluru, enjoyed the convenience of money. Gone were the days of cash. Swipes, taps, and clicks; his world made him revolve.

It started innocently. His father provided him with a debit card, which he could use in case of an emergency. However, soon Aarav began to use it for online shopping, food delivery, and cabs. The sense of having money without the physical cash in his wallet made him feel he had an unlimited amount of money.

When "Buy Now, Pay Later" offers appeared on his favorite shopping apps, he thought it was the smartest hack ever. "Why pay today when I can pay next month?" he told himself. Soon, he was juggling multiple BNPL bills, each one promising "zero interest" but hitting him with hidden charges when he missed deadlines.

Crypto ads flooded his social media feeds, showing young influencers flaunting luxury cars and telling him that "Bitcoin is the future." Without research, Aarav poured his savings into whatever coin was trending. Within months, half of it evaporated when the market crashed.

Then came the Insta-loan apps. He borrowed ₹15,000 to clear one BNPL bill, thinking he'd pay it back quickly. But high interest rates snowballed, and he found himself in a cycle of borrowing one loan to pay another.

The worst part? Aarav ignored red flags. He clicked on phishing links disguised as "UPI cashback offers" and lost ₹5,000 in a scam. Embarrassed, he didn't tell anyone, just borrowed again to cover it up.

By 24, Aarav was drowning in digital debt. His credit score tanked. Banks refused him even a basic credit card. The convenience that felt empowering at first had turned into chains. Aarav wasn't living the digital money dream; he was trapped in a digital money maze.

Aarav's story isn't rare. Many youngsters fall into the same traps because digital money feels less "real" than cash. The convenience hides the cost. This chapter is about untangling that maze, learning how to enjoy the power of digital finance without letting it control you.

The Illusion of Money with Swipes and Taps

When you hand over cash, you feel the weight of spending. When you swipe a card or scan a QR code, the money disappears invisibly. Psychologically, this makes overspending easier.

For young people just starting to earn or manage money, this illusion is dangerous.

- Ordering food feels cheap until you check the end-of-month total.

- Splitting bills digitally feels smooth, but it adds up.
- The "tap-and-go" culture makes you underestimate how much you're actually spending.

Tip: Make money visible. Use apps that categorize your spending. Seeing that you spent ₹8,000 on food deliveries in one month hits harder than watching a dozen ₹199 payments slide past.

New-Age Traps Young People Fall Into

1. BNPL (Buy Now, Pay Later)

It looks harmless: buy shoes today, pay next month. But here's the catch:

- Miss a deadline, and penalties shoot up.
- Multiple BNPL accounts create confusion, as you forget when each payment is due.
- It tricks you into thinking you can afford more than you actually can.

Rule: If you can't pay it today, don't buy it on BNPL.

2. Insta-Loans

Loan apps advertise instant approvals with minimal checks. Tempting, right? But the interest rates are often brutal, sometimes disguised in fine print.

- Borrowing ₹10,000 might mean paying back ₹15,000 in a few months.

- Miss a payment, and harassment begins, calls, messages, even threats.

Rule: Never borrow for lifestyle expenses. Loans are for emergencies, not impulse buys.

3. Crypto Hype

Crypto is not evil, but diving in without research is financial suicide. Many youngsters invest because of FOMO (fear of missing out) or flashy influencer promotions.

- Markets are volatile; what doubles today can halve tomorrow.
- Scams thrive on hype, fake coins, pump-and-dump schemes, and rug pulls.

Rule: Never invest money in crypto that you can't afford to lose.

4. FOMO Investing

It's not just crypto. Stocks, NFTs, even random apps promise "guaranteed returns." Young people, especially students and first-jobbers, jump in without basics.

- Chasing quick gains often means ignoring risks.
- Panic buying and panic selling wipe out savings.

Rule: Slow wealth is real wealth. Quick shortcuts usually cut your future short.

Digital Banking and Safety

For every benefit of UPI and digital wallets, there's a scam lurking. Young people, being the heaviest users, are also the softest targets.

Common traps:

- Fake cashback links → drain your account.
- Fraud calls posing as bank representatives.
- Sharing OTPs out of panic or confusion.

Red Flags:

- Anyone asking for your OTP is a scammer.
- No bank ever asks you to "click a link to verify details."
- If it feels urgent and pushy, it's probably fake.

Healthy Usage of Fintech Apps

Not all apps are traps. Used wisely, they can become your best allies.

- Budgeting apps: Track spending patterns.
- Savings automation: Round up your payments and put spare change into savings.
- Credit score check tools: Help you monitor your financial health early.

The trick is using apps consciously, not mindlessly.

Responsible Digital Behavior

Treat your digital wallet like your physical one:

- Don't leave it open for anyone to access.
- Don't load it with money you can't afford to lose.
- Set limits for yourself, weekly or monthly caps on online spending.

Golden Rule: If you wouldn't do it with cash, don't do it digitally.

Why Digital Money Feels So Different?

Young people today rarely touch physical cash. A tap, a swipe, or a QR scan feels effortless, but this ease creates blind spots.

Psychologists call this "spending invisibility." When you hand over ₹500, you feel the loss. When you tap to pay ₹500, your brain barely registers it. Multiply this dozens of times in a week, and you've spent thousands without realizing it.

For someone earning their first stipend or salary, this illusion is dangerous. The less "real" money feels, the faster it slips away.

Quick Fix: Create a system that makes spending visible. Use apps that give you weekly summaries. Even writing expenses in a notebook helps. Awareness is your first shield.

The Reality Behind BNPL (Buy Now, Pay Later)

BNPL looks like magic: order something now, pay later, no questions asked. But here's what actually happens:

- You feel rich for a few days, but the bill arrives when you least expect it.
- Miss a deadline? The penalties are far harsher than you think.
- Too many BNPL purchases lead to confusion; suddenly, you're juggling multiple repayment dates.

Real Example: Rhea, a 21-year-old, bought clothes, shoes, and gadgets through three different BNPL apps. By the end of the month, she had five payment reminders and not enough money to cover them. She paid one, delayed the others, and her credit score tanked before she even applied for her first credit card.

Lesson: BNPL is a trap if you use it for lifestyle purchases. If you can't pay today, don't buy it.

The Dark Side of Insta-Loans

Loan apps make borrowing money feel as easy as ordering pizza. Just a few taps, and you get ₹10,000 in your account. But behind the slick design is a debt trap.

- Interest rates are disguised. What looks like a 2% monthly charge is really 24% a year.
- If you delay repayment, penalties skyrocket.
- Some apps even harass borrowers, calling friends, spamming contacts, and shaming them online.

Real Example: Aditya, a 23-year-old engineering graduate, borrowed ₹15,000 from an app to cover rent. He couldn't repay on time. By the third month, the app demanded ₹28,000. When he hesitated, they began calling his relatives. His mental health crashed.

Lesson: Loans should never fund lifestyle gaps. If you're using them for wants, not needs, you're already in trouble.

Crypto Hype and FOMO Investing

Crypto and new-age investments attract young people with promises of quick riches. Social media influencers flaunt Lamborghinis, telling you "this coin will 10x."

But here's the truth:

- Crypto is highly volatile. Values can drop 50% overnight.
- Many "projects" are scams, rug pulls, fake coins, and pump-and-dump schemes.
- Investing blindly because of FOMO (fear of missing out) usually ends in losses.

Real Example: Simran, a 20-year-old college student, put her savings of ₹40,000 into a trendy coin after a YouTuber hyped it. Within two weeks, it lost 70% of its value. The influencer had already cashed out, leaving followers trapped.

Lesson: Never invest money you can't afford to lose. Build knowledge before risking money.

How Scams Catch Young People

Digital fraudsters target young users because they're always online. Common tricks include:

- Fake cashback links that drain accounts.
- Calls pretending to be from banks.
- Fraudsters offering "instant credit boosts" or "free gifts" in exchange for OTPs.

Red Flags:

- No bank will ever ask for your OTP.
- If someone creates urgency ("Act now or your account will freeze"), it's almost always fake.
- If a deal looks too good to be true, it usually is.

Rule: Think twice before clicking. Scammers prey on speed; your weapon is patience.

Fintech Apps – The Good Side

Not all apps are bad. Some can actually help you become smarter with money.

- Budgeting tools: Apps like Walnut or Mint categorize expenses automatically, showing where your money goes.
- Savings automation: Features that round up every spend and transfer the extra to savings.

- Credit score apps: Help you track your CIBIL score early so you don't ruin it before needing a loan.

The key difference: These apps help you grow, not trap you.

Responsible Digital Habits

Think of digital money like a sharp tool; it's powerful if you know how to use it, dangerous if you don't.

Tips for Young Users:

1. Set weekly or monthly spending caps in your payment apps.
2. Keep only what you plan to use in wallets; don't preload huge amounts.
3. Check your bank notifications daily, catch small frauds before they grow.
4. Use strong passwords and never repeat the same one across apps.

Golden Question: Before every digital spend, ask yourself: Would I still buy this if I had to pay cash for it right now?

Building Your Digital Money Toolkit

Digital money isn't the enemy; it's how you use it that matters. With the right approach, your phone can become a personal finance coach instead of a debt trap. Here's how to build a toolkit that works for you.

Step 1: Track, Don't Just Transact

Most youngsters treat UPI apps only as payment tools, not learning tools. But every transaction leaves a trail.

- Go through your monthly transaction history.
- Categorize: food, travel, subscriptions, shopping, etc.
- Notice patterns, are food deliveries swallowing half your budget?

Framework:

Awareness → Control → Growth

First, see where the money is going. Then, set caps for categories. Finally, redirect savings into investments.

The goal isn't to stop spending; it's to spend consciously.

Step 2: Treat BNPL Like a Loan

BNPL feels harmless because apps don't call it "debt." But it is debt. Every "pay later" is money borrowed from your future self.

- Before you click "pay later," ask: Would I take a loan for this purchase?
- If the answer is no, don't use BNPL.
- Keep track of all repayment dates in one place; missed deadlines are silent killers.

Remember, your credit score starts building the moment you enter adulthood. Protect it now.

Step 3: Say No to Insta-Loans (Unless It's an Emergency)

There's nothing wrong with borrowing in emergencies. But when loans become a shortcut for lifestyle upgrades, you dig yourself into a hole.

- If you need money for essentials, borrow from family first, interest-free.
- If you must use a loan app, read the fine print carefully.
- Never stack loans (borrowing from one app to pay another). That's how spirals begin.

Step 4: Handle Crypto with Caution

Crypto and new-age assets can be exciting, but don't let FOMO control you.

- Research before you invest. Read whitepapers, not just influencer tweets.
- Start with tiny amounts, money you can afford to lose.
- Never put emergency savings or rent money into crypto.

Golden Rule: Crypto can be a part of your portfolio, not your entire portfolio.

Step 5: Build Cyber-Smart Habits

Digital finance is safe only if you're smart. A single careless click can drain months of savings.

- Double-check URLs before entering banking details.

- Never share OTPs, not with friends, not with "bank officials," not with anyone.
- Avoid public Wi-Fi for financial transactions.
- Use two-factor authentication wherever possible.

Think of cybersecurity as hygiene. It is like crossing the street. You don't be careful once and forget; you do it each time. Same with digital safety.

A Framework for Responsible Digital Spending

Let's simplify responsible digital behavior into a 3–2–1 system:

3 questions before every spend:

1. Do I need this?
2. Can I afford it today (not later)?
3. Am I buying it for me, or to impress others?

2 tools to track every month:

1. Expense tracker (manual or app).
2. Bank statement review.

1 rule to stick to:

1. Spend less than you earn, always. Digital convenience doesn't change this.

Red Flags Youngsters Must Watch For

1. **Too Many Apps, Too Many Accounts**

   Juggling four BNPL apps, two wallets, and a loan app is a recipe for disaster. Keep things simple, fewer apps, clearer control.

2. **Impulse Buying with One Tap**

   If you feel the urge to buy instantly, force a 24-hour pause. Most cravings vanish.

3. **Subscriptions You Forgot About**

   Gym apps, OTT, courses, and small debits add up. Audit subscriptions every few months.

4. **Blind Trust in Influencers**

   Just because someone flaunts a car on Instagram doesn't mean their financial advice is sound. Always cross-check.

5. **Ignoring Credit Scores**

   A bad score today will haunt you tomorrow when you need a loan for education, travel, or business.

Turning Fintech into Your Ally

Used with discipline, digital tools can become your strength:

- Budget apps keep you accountable.
- Auto-savings grow your wealth silently.
- UPI alerts protect against fraud.

- Credit score apps give early warnings.

The difference is mindset: are you using these tools, or are they using you?

Why Discipline Matters More Than Technology?

Every generation faces money traps. For your parents, it was credit cards. For you, it's BNPL and UPI. The tools change, but the principle doesn't: discipline beats convenience.

You can't stop the world from becoming cashless. But you can stop yourself from becoming careless.

The Cultural Pull of Digital Money

Digital payments have changed how young Indians live, not just how they spend. Swiping, scanning, and tapping aren't just about convenience; they're tied to identity, lifestyle, and belonging.

From group dinners split on UPI to "gifting" through apps on birthdays, digital money is woven into social life. But with it comes pressure: if everyone is paying instantly, buying instantly, living instantly, you feel like you need to keep up.

That's where problems begin.

Peer Pressure in a Cashless Era

In the past, peer pressure was about owning branded shoes or the latest phone. Today, it's about:

- Splurging at trendy cafés because everyone pays via wallet apps.

- Booking cabs daily because UPI makes it "only ₹200."
- Upgrading gadgets because EMI options pop up as soon as you browse.

Digital ease makes resisting harder. You don't feel the pinch of parting with notes; you just feel the buzz of belonging.

How to Resist Without Feeling Left Out:

- Suggest budget-friendly hangouts. Real friends won't care where you meet.
- Be upfront about limits: "I'm saving this month, so I'll skip that plan."
- Use shared expense apps to keep fairness in group spending.

You don't have to keep pace with others' spending to keep their friendship.

Lifestyle Inflation in the Digital Age

Lifestyle inflation is when your spending grows as your income grows. In the digital era, it's on steroids.

- Got a salary hike? Your favorite shopping app already has offers waiting.
- Just received your stipend? Food delivery apps start sending "treat yourself" notifications.

The ease of digital spending makes lifestyle creep invisible. You start feeling that upgrades are normal, not luxuries.

Break the Cycle:

- Keep your fixed costs low, rent, EMI, and subscriptions.
- For every income increase, save at least half before adjusting lifestyle.
- Celebrate progress by building assets, not liabilities.

The Social Media Factor

Social media is fuel for the digital money maze. Flashy reels of vacations, gadgets, and "trader lifestyles" create FOMO. You feel broke not because you are, but because you're comparing yourself to curated highlights.

How to Detox from Comparison:

- Remind yourself: people post successes, not debts.
- Follow creators who talk about financial discipline, not just luxury.
- Challenge yourself to post your own wins, like saving ₹10,000 or investing your first SIP.

Money confidence grows when you celebrate your own progress, not when you chase someone else's.

Why Overspending Feels "Normal" Digitally?

Spending digitally feels less risky because:

- Payments are fast, invisible, and often delayed.
- Apps gamify spending with rewards, cashback, and coins.

- Your brain processes numbers differently when they're abstract, not physical.

But here's the truth: ₹5000 spent online is still ₹5000 gone. Rewards don't erase real costs.

Tip: Before buying, calculate how many hours of work that expense equals. Suddenly, a ₹2000 impulsive purchase feels heavier if it's a full day's effort.

Balancing Digital Life and Financial Health

You don't have to reject digital money; it's the future. The key is balance.

- Use cash once in a while to "feel" money again. It makes you value it.
- Switch off notifications that push you to spend.
- Keep a "wish list" rule, add to cart, wait 48 hours, then decide.

Balance means enjoying convenience without losing control.

The New Definition of Cool

For many youngsters, "cool" means showing off a new gadget or dining at fancy places. But the real flex in today's digital world is:

- Paying bills on time.
- Having savings despite temptations.
- Saying no to debt traps.

- Using fintech for growth, not destruction.

Shift your definition of cool, and suddenly, peer pressure loses its power.

Why This Matters Now

At your age, you are getting exposed to a full digital financial world. That means:

- You'll make more financial decisions through apps than banks.
- Scams and traps will target you more than anyone else.
- Your digital habits will shape your entire financial future.

That's why mastering the maze isn't optional; it's survival.

Meera's Digital Discipline

Meera, a 24-year-old marketing executive in Delhi, loved technology as much as anyone else her age. She ordered food online, paid with UPI, and even invested through apps. But unlike many of her peers, Meera had one golden rule: use digital tools, don't let them use you.

When she got her first salary, she didn't rush into BNPL offers. Instead, she linked her account to a budgeting app. At the end of every week, she reviewed her spending categories: food, travel, shopping, and subscriptions. Seeing the totals in one place made her conscious of habits.

She avoided BNPL for lifestyle shopping. Her logic was simple: "If I can't afford it today, I probably don't need it." By sticking to this, she stayed debt-free.

Crypto tempted her too. Friends bragged about their "moonshot coins," but Meera spent weeks reading articles, watching explainer videos, and learning the basics before putting in a small amount, money she was willing to lose. The rest of her savings went into SIPs and a fixed emergency fund.

Scams? She was alert. A stranger once sent her a "cashback link," but she remembered her rule: no bank ever asks for clicks or OTPs. She ignored it and reported the number.

Even in social situations, she handled peer pressure smartly. When friends suggested expensive outings, she'd offer alternatives, game nights, potlucks, and budget-friendly cafés. Nobody felt left out, and her savings grew steadily.

By 25, Meera had what most of her peers lacked:

- A healthy savings habit.
- Zero digital debt.
- A good credit score.
- Peace of mind that no scam or sudden expense could ruin her.

A Tale of Two Choices

Compare Meera's life with Aarav's.

- Aarav swiped without thinking, fell into BNPL and loan traps, and wrecked his credit score.
- Meera used the same apps, but with discipline, awareness, and self-control.

Both had the same opportunities, the same digital tools. The difference was in mindset.

Your Takeaway

Digital money is here to stay. The question is, will you let it control you, or will you master it?

- Don't fall for the illusion of easy swipes and taps.
- Avoid traps like BNPL debt cycles and shady loan apps.
- Treat crypto and FOMO investing with caution.
- Use fintech apps as allies for budgeting, saving, and credit health.
- Stay alert against scams and fraud.

The future belongs to those who use digital tools responsibly. You don't have to reject convenience; you just have to pair it with discipline.

Aarav's story is the warning. Meera's story is the inspiration. Your story? That's still being written.

Every time you scan, swipe, or click, you're choosing which path to walk. Will you get lost in the maze, or will you navigate it with clarity?

If you take one lesson from this chapter, let it be this: in the cashless world, the smartest currency is awareness.

Chapter 8: Constructing Your Financial Plan – From Confusion to Clarity

Karan's Chaos

Karan was 25, employed at a tech startup in Hyderabad. On paper, he was fine, good salary, hot social scene, and the latest gadgets at his fingertips. But in terms of money, Karan was the epitome of confusion.

Each month, his pay would find its way to his account and be gone just as fast. Rent, grocery delivery, weekend getaways, bike EMIs, and spontaneous shopping online. By the third week of the month, he was taking money from friends.

He never accounted for where his money went. Budgeting was so tedious. Insurance? He believed that was something only "old people" did. Emergency fund? "My parents will bail me out if something goes wrong."

When his company offered health insurance, he ignored the details. When friends discussed investments, he brushed it off: "I'll think about it later."

But "later" arrived earlier than anticipated. An unexpected medical crisis in his household compelled him to pay ₹60,000 in advance. He had saved nothing. No insurance. No strategy. He dipped into his credit card, availed himself of a small personal loan, and convinced himself that he would cope. But when the repayments began, he realized he had gotten himself trapped in a cycle of debt.

Karan's bewilderment became anxiety. He made good money but had no direction, no purpose, and no financial security blanket. Each financial setback was like a knockout blow.

Karan's experience is a reminder: money does not take care of itself. Without a plan, a good income feels like sand running through your fingers. This chapter is about shifting that chaos into clarity, creating your own financial map.

Creating Your Personal Money Map

A money map is just what the name says: a map that indicates where you are financially, where you want to be, and how you will get there.

Here's what you put in it:

Income: Know precisely how much you take home after tax. That's your real buying power.

Expenses: Divide them into needs (rent, food, transport), wants (shopping, eating out), and savings.

Goals: Short-term (new computer, holiday), medium-term (more studies, marriage, car), long-term (house, retirement).

Risks: Consider what might blow you off course: job loss, health, and emergencies.

Safety Net: Emergency fund, insurance, and savings that catch you.

The money map is not a single exercise; it's dynamic with your life.

Planning for Life Events

Life contains milestones: education, marriage, travel, and home purchase. If you don't plan, they all feel like a financial earthquake. If you do plan, they're manageable.

Higher Education: If you wish to study overseas, begin saving early. Even SIPs of small amounts can sum up to a significant amount over 2–3 years.

Marriage: Rather than going for loans or relying on the family, plan your contribution. Begin your married life without debt.

Travel: Build a "travel fund." Save a little every month rather than using your card at the last moment.

Home: A house is a large aspiration. Don't hurry, though. First, build an emergency fund, then make down payments.

Emergencies: These are not negotiable; they canoccur. Medical problems, loss of job, accidents. Without a fund, you'll go underwater in loans.

The objective is straightforward: when life events occur, you need to be prepared, not panicked.

The Safety Net: Insurance and Emergency Funds

Youngsterstend to believe that insurance is dull or unnecessary. But here's the reality:

- Medical insurance shields you from those hospital bills that can destroy savings.
- Term insurance safeguards your family from being financially ruined if anything happens to you.
- Emergency funds are also vital. Shoot for 3–6 months' worth of expenses in a liquid account. That's your cushion against the unknown.

Frame insurance and emergency funds as your financial helmet. You don't wear a helmet because you anticipate an accident; you wear it because accidents are unexpected.

Financial Freedom vs. Simply Being "Financially Free"

Most people believe financial freedom is "I get paid good, I can spend as I please." That's not freedom, that's vulnerability.

Financially free = No urgent deficit of funds.

Financial freedom = Being able to live life on your own terms without debt or anxiety.

Actual freedom is when:

- You can leave a bad job without freaking out.
- You can go on break for studies or vacation because you've saved.
- You can deal with emergencies without begging or borrowing.

It's not luxury; it's control.

Mini Challenges to Begin Taking Control

Theory is useless without execution. Here are easy challenges you can begin today:

Track 30 Days of Spending: Record every rupee you spend. Awareness is step one.

Save Your First Emergency Fund (Equal to at least 3 months of your expenses): Don't even think of touching it unless it's a true emergency.

Begin One SIP: Even ₹500 a month creates the habit of investing.

Check Your Digital Subscriptions: Unsubscribe from what you don't use.

Learn One New Money Concept Each Week: CIBIL, inflation, compound interest, and information grow like money.

A Step-By-Step Framework to Move Towards Financial Freedom

Here's a step-by-step approach to ensure that you're not just financially free, but are instead living with the financial freedom you desire in life.

Step 1: Know Your Real Income

Many young people get CTC (Cost to Company) and take-home pay mixed up. Your actual income is the real money that reaches your bank account after deducting taxes, provident fund (PF), and other deductions. Note that PF is one of the best-in-class financial instruments that grows with your and your employer's monthly contribution, with interest added to your capital every year.

Example: Your CTC could be ₹6 lakh a year, but your take-home might be more like ₹38,000 a month.

Unless you know this, you'll always overestimate your spending power.

Action: Take your payslip, dissect it, and note the actual take-home amount. That's what you budget with.

Step 2: Break Down Expenses

There are three categories of expenses:

1. **Needs** – rent, food, transport, and internet.
2. **Wants** – new clothes, gadgets, and eating out.
3. **Savings/Investments** – cash you set aside for the future.

For the majority of young adults, wants override because needs are unexciting. But without intention, your wage will vanish quicker than you realize.

Action: Utilize the 50–30–20 rule:

50% on needs

30% on wants

20% on savings

Even if you can't achieve these specific percentages, the idea is to save first before indulging. Don't have the mindset of saving what is left. Instead save first and plan with what is left.

Step 3: Define Your Goals

Without objectives, money trickles into useless expenditures. Objectives provide direction for your money.

Short-term (0–2 years): Upgrade laptop, vacation, online course.

Medium-term (3–5 years): Master's outside the country, car down payment, marriage, side business.

Long-term (5+ years): Home purchase, financial freedom, retirement plan.

Action: Set three goals, one short, one medium, one long. Assign a number and time frame to each. Example: "Save ₹1.5 lakh in 2 years for a Europe trip."

Step 4: Identify Risks

Risks are what can blow your plan apart. For young people, these are the big ones:

- Sudden job loss.
- Medical emergencies (for you or for family members).
- Debt spirals using credit cards/loans.

Action: Ask yourself, "If this risk hit me tomorrow, how would I handle it?" If your answer is "borrow," you need a safety net.

Step 5: Build a Safety Net

A safety net = emergency fund + insurance.

Emergency fund: At least 3 months of your essential expenses, held in a savings account or liquid fund. Don't invest it long-term; you need instant access.

Insurance:

1. **Health insurance:** Even if your employer provides it, take a personal one as well.
2. **Term insurance:** If others are reliant on your income, this is not optional.

Think of these as armor. They do not make you wealthy, but they prevent you from becoming impoverished overnight.

Practical Example: Arjun's Money Map

Arjun is 23, takes home ₹35,000 per month.

Needs: ₹18,000 (rent, food, transport).

Wants: 9000 (dining out, subscriptions).

Savings: ₹8,000.

Goals:

Short term: Buy a new phone for ₹30,000 and save ₹5,000/month in 6 months.

Medium term: ₹2 lakh as application fee in a foreign country for Master's - SIP ₹6000/month in 3 years.

Long term: ₹10 lakh in 7 years - invest in mutual funds ₹5,000/month.

Safety net:

Emergency fund: ₹1 lakh goal → save ₹4,000/month until fully done.

Health insurance: ₹5 lakh coverage outside his company's coverage.

With this clarity, Arjun is not scared of surprises. His money map leads him.

The Worst Error: Navigation Without a Map

The majority of young adults procrastinate regarding finances because they believe:

"I don't make enough yet."

"I'll deal with it later."

But money behavior begins when you're broke, not when you're wealthy. The sooner you chart your money, the quicker you become free.

Preparing for Life Events Without Panic

Life is filled with milestones, some planned, others not. Unless you plan ahead, each one is a financial earthquake. With even a simple plan, you'll meet them with calm rather than chaos.

1. Higher Education

For others in their early 20s, pursuing higher studies, either in India or overseas, is on the wish list. But wishes don't come cheap.

Tuition fees, application fees, exam fees (like GRE, IELTS), and living expenses mount quickly.

Holding on only to education loans is to begin your professional life in debt.

Bright Idea:

- Save while in college or in your initial job, even if it's only ₹2,000 a month.
- Utilize SIPs in mutual funds for 2–5 year time frames.
- Create a small "education fund" ahead of applying; it lowers how much you have to borrow.

2. Marriage

Indian weddings are renowned for money burning. Adolescents tend to feel obligated to overspend due to family or societal pressures.

Smart Move:

- Set priorities, intimacy, or splurges.
- Make an early budget and be rigid with it.
- Don't take out wedding loans; debt is a bad way to begin married life.
- Save every month for a minimum of 2–3 years if you desire to splurge.

Remember: a wedding is but a day; marriage is forever.

3. Travel Plans

Each teenager has a fantasy of seeing the globe, or even just taking that Goa trip with friends. The catch? Most swipe their credit card or use BNPL for "vacation deals."

Smart Move:

- Create a "travel fund." Even ₹100 per day totals more than ₹30,000 per year.
- Have a different account or wallet so you won't tap into it by mistake.
- Take trips based on offers and off-peak seasons rather than peak frenzy periods.

Travel tastes sweeter when you know you won't be paying it off months down the line.

4. Home Buying

Purchasing a home as a 20-something feels like the pinnacle of adulthood. But moving too quickly can have negative consequences.

Loans can hold you captive for 20 years.

A home must be an option, not a drag.

Smart Move:

- First, establish a solid emergency fund.
- Save up at least 20% of the down payment before even looking at a loan.

- Don't let peers or family influence you; purchase when it makes sense for you, not for show.

5. Emergencies

This is the one milestone no one discusses, but everyone experiences. Sickness, accidents, loss of a job, they don't come with notice.

Smart Move:

- Have at least 3–6 months of living costs in an emergency fund.
- Keep it out of sight from everyday savings, don't use it for shopping or vacations.
- Ensure you and your family have sufficient health insurance.

An emergency fund does not make you wealthy, but it prevents you from becoming poor overnight.

The Safety Net: Insurance

Insurance is not fear, it's planning. A lot of young adults disregard it, believing it's something for "later." However, later usually arrives too late.

Health Insurance: One hospital bill can blow years of savings away. Don't just count on company cover; it disappears if you leave.

Term Insurance: If your loved ones rely on your paycheck, this is not negotiable. It's inexpensive when you're young.

Consider insurance your financial seatbelt. You never intend to crash, but you always use one.

Balancing Goals Without Stress

The secret is not doing everything at once. Prioritize.

1. First: Emergency fund + health insurance.
2. Next: Short-term goals (education, vacation).
3. Then: Medium/long-term goals (marriage, home).

Don't spread yourself too thin pursuing all at the same time. Do it step by step, slow but sure.

Mini Challenge: The "Goal Jar"

To make saving for goals entertaining, try this:

1. Have three jars (or three virtual wallets). Label them "Education," "Travel," "Emergency."
2. Deposit something in each jar each month, no matter how small.
3. See them grow.

The visual gauging keeps you encouraged.

Financial Freedom vs. Just Being "Financially Free"

Most young people mix getting well paid with financial freedom. Having cash available today does not necessarily make you secure in the future.

Financially free means you can afford what you desire right now or take independent financial decisions.

Financial freedom is a state of doing life the way you want without having to stress, get into debt, or be dependent.

Example: Karan earns 60,000 a month. Every half a year, he writes about new devices, goes out to restaurants daily, and posts pictures of weekend trips. It looks like he has been released to his friends. However, when his employer delays two months' salaries, he has no reserve. Abruptly, his lifestyle ends.

Compare that with Arjun, who earns the same but saves periodically, has an emergency corpus, and invests in SIP. He is not in a panic when his company is laying off its employees; his financial independence offers options.

Learning point: Money does not make one financially free, but good habits do.

Mini Challenges to Build Your Blueprint

Theory is good only if you apply it. Here are real-life challenges meant for youth to begin building discipline from day one.

Challenge 1: The 30-Day Expense Diary

For thirty days, record every single thing you spend, no matter how small, like ₹50 on tea. Afterward, examine:

1. Where did you spend most of your cash?
2. What expenses brought you genuine happiness?
3. Which were only impulses?

Knowing is the first step to clarity.

Challenge 2: The First ₹10,000 Emergency Fund

Make it your goal to save your first ₹10,000. Slow and steady works. ₹100 a day will get you there in a little over 3 months.

This money is not for shopping or "sales." It's your emergency fund.

Challenge 3: Cancel and Redirect

Go through all your subscriptions, OTT, courses, and apps. Unsubscribe from what you don't use. Channel that money into savings.

Example: Three unused subscriptions for ₹500/month = ₹1,500/month → ₹18,000/year. That's nearly a new laptop, simply by cutting waste.

Challenge 4: One SIP, No Excuses

Begin a tiny SIP (even ₹500/month). It's less than a pizza night out, but over 5 years, it creates the habit of wealth creation.

Don't wait to do it when you have the "perfect" salary. Begin with what you have.

Challenge 5: Learn the Lingo

Each week, choose one money term: CIBIL score, inflation, compound interest, mutual fund, or term insurance. Learn about it, know it, and educate a friend.

Knowledge grows like money; the sooner you begin, the wealthier you become.

Why These Challenges Succeed

Each of these bite-sized steps builds momentum. They're small enough not to overwhelm but significant enough to change habits.

- Tracking → awareness.
- Emergency fund → security.
- Cancel & redirect → discipline.
- SIP → growth mindset.
- Learning lingo → confidence.

Both of them are the backbone of your financial plan.

From Confusion to Clarity

Money confusion is a result of two things: not having information and not taking action. Clarity results from action, even small ones.

You don't have to be a guru or make lakhs to create stability. You just need:

1. Awareness of how your money is going.
2. A plan for where you want it to go.
3. The discipline to stick with it.

Arjun's Clarity

Arjun is a 24-year-old graphic designer based in Pune who was not earning such a huge amount of money, but he was skilled enough to make every rupee count. He was different from Karan in that he never left his money to fate. He created his own money map early on.

He updated his monthly income and expenditure in an easy spreadsheet.

He split his salary between needs, wants, and savings, never missing the savings component.

He maintained a modest emergency fund of ₹50,000 prior to splurging on his first high-priced gadget.

When his friends went on spending sprees with BNPL, he steered clear of the trap: "If I can't afford it today, I'll wait."

He began a ₹1,500 SIP with his first salary.

When life threw curves, Arjun was prepared. An unexpected medical bill did not faze him; it was covered by his insurance. When his firm held back wages in a bad quarter, he coped because of his emergency fund.

Arjun wasn't making more than anyone else, but he lived with poise and tranquility. His clarity provided him with freedom.

The Contrast

Karan: Made well but lacked clarity → went into debt and panic.

Arjun: Worked moderately but had a plan → lived life with confidence.

Both had equal opportunities. Money was not the difference; it was mindset and discipline.

Your Financial Blueprint: The Essentials

Going forward, remember the following pillars of clarity:

1. Keep track of revenues and costs honestly.
2. Separate needs, wants, and savings.
3. Establish short, medium, and long-term objectives.
4. Develop an emergency fund (safety net).
5. Invest small but regularly.
6. Keep studying, finance is a lifetime skill.

Financial Freedom: Your True Goal

Don't pursue the fantasy of being "financially free" right now. Pursue actual financial freedom: making decisions without fear. That's when you can say no to garbage jobs, yes to deals, and live on your terms.

Mini Blueprint Challenge

Before you set this book down, do this today:

1. Write your monthly income.
2. Write your average expenses.
3. Write one short-term and one long-term goal.
4. Save a minimum of ₹500 this week towards those targets.

Small starts make big differences.

A Final Message

Money isn't about figures; it's about clarity, decisions, and guts. Many young people fall into financial pitfalls because nobody handed them the map. That's why this book was written – to provide you with that map, step by step.

Remember: You don't have to be wealthy to begin; you have to begin to become wealthy. Discipline today turns into freedom tomorrow. Success isn't quantified by how much you spend but by how much control you have.

A Letter to The Reader

Dear reader,

If you've read this far, you already are different. You've opted for awareness versus ignorance, clarity versus confusion. It is not going to be a perfect money path, and you are going to make mistakes. However, with the right mindset and roadmap, you will recover faster and become tougher.

Be like Arjun, not Karan. Cultivate habits, not debt. Seek liberty, not form.

And first and foremost, never forget: money is a means and not a trap. Properly used, it will lead you to the life you want.

Bonus Chapter: Money Beyond Basics – Your Guide to Smarter Investing

Aarav's Comfortable Illusion

Aarav was 26 and an employee of a well-known IT firm in Pune. His father had always advised him, "Invest your money in a fixed deposit. It's safe. It's guaranteed."

Aarav did just that. Every bonus he received, he invested in an FD.

He boasted to his friends, "I do not believe in risk. At least my money is safe."

Three years later, he viewed his FD receipts with satisfaction. His interest accrued plus principal had increased by 18%.

Meanwhile, during the same period, he observed a curious thing: his spending had also increased.

The rent was more.

Milk and vegetables almost doubled in cost.

Weekend lunches with his friends, which were ₹300 per person before, now never dropped below ₹600.

It was then that reality hit: while his cash was theoretically increasing, its value was declining. The 18% return in three years didn't really create wealth; it barely kept up. Indeed, after deducting taxes from the FD interest, Aarav realized that he was actually losing ground.

For the first time, he realized that being too cautious could be dangerous in itself.

"Saving is Equal to Earning" – The Time-Honoured Aphorism That Remains Applicable

There's a reason why elderly people like to say this: "Bachhat karna hi kamai karne jaisa hai" (saving is as good as earning).

Why? Because saving each rupee means you don't have to earn it again.

Consider this:

If you earn ₹1,000 and spend the entire amount, you are left with ₹0.

If you save ₹200 of that, it's as if you earned an additional ₹200 without putting in additional effort.

Savings are unspoken income. They do not appear in your salary slip, but they build your financial foundation.

Let us consider a simple example:

Ravi earns ₹30,000 per month and spends ₹28,000. Saving = ₹2,000.

Sunil earns ₹25,000 per month but spends only ₹20,000. Saving = ₹5,000.

Who's wealthier? In theory, Ravi is wealthier since he earns more. But in practice, Sunil is accumulating more money since his savings are greater.

Fact is: earning more is not the key; it's saving better.

Reflection Question: When you hear about your income, do you simply compute your wage, or do you also compute how much you save?

Inflation – The Quiet Wealth Destroyer

If savings are income, then inflation is the unseen cost we readily overlook.

Inflation is just this: the creeping cost of goods and services with time.

A cinema ticket, which was ₹120 a few years ago, could now be ₹250.

A kilogram of rice, which was ₹40, could now be ₹65.

A family meal, which was ₹1,000, can now easily breach ₹2,000.

This consistent increase nibbles at the worth of money.

Here's a wake-up call: If India's inflation averages 6% per annum (which it does over the long term to a rough approximation), then ₹100 kept today will only be worth approximately ₹56 in a decade. That's nearly half its strength lost!

And when folks say, "I keep my money safe in a bank," they overlook the fact that the money is not actually safe; it's quietly diminishing.

The Real Danger:

FD at 5.5% – Tax at 20% – Net return = 4.4%

Inflation = 6%

Real Growth = –1.6% (a loss in purchasing power!)

Inflation is like a slow leak in your financial bucket. If your investments don't outpace it, you'll find yourself running harder just to stand still.

Reflection Question: Have you ever noticed your favorite snack or coffee becoming pricier over the years?

Now, imagine your savings remaining constant while the world around you becomes costly. How long will your money actually last?

Why Investments Need to Beat Inflation

Imagine you are running a race where the ground you are running on keeps shifting backward. That's what inflation does to your money.

If your income increases at 5% but inflation increases at 6%, you are actually becoming poorer, yet the figure in your payslip appears larger.

That's why beating inflation is the bare minimum that any investment should meet.

Consider Aarav's example of FD:

He invested ₹1,00,000 in an FD at 6% for 3 years.

Inflation over those 3 years was 6% per annum.

After tax, his FD returned him an effective 4.5%.

Real return = –1.5% annually.

So, whereas his money "grew" to ₹1,19,000, in real buying power terms, it was able to buy less than what the ₹1,00,000 could three years ago.

This is the reason why wealth is not a matter of how much you save, but how wisely you invest.

When you are investing in assets such as equities, mutual funds, or index funds that traditionally return 10–12% in the long term, not only are you increasing your money, you are ahead of inflation.

Key Lesson: Your money must work harder than inflation. You're just running in place if not.

Why FD Alone Isn't an Investment

Let's be frank: Fixed Deposits (FDs) are not evil. They offer:

- Safety (capital protection)
- Liquidity (easy withdrawal)
- Predictability (fixed interest rate)

But the problem is, they are often mistaken for investments when in reality, they are just parking spaces for money.

Why FD falls short as an "investment":

- Low returns: Rarely beats inflation after tax.
- Taxable interest: Interest earned is fully taxed as income.
- Opportunity cost: While your money sits in an FD, it misses the chance to grow faster elsewhere.

Remember FD as a safety locker. It's secure, but does a locker increase your wealth? No, it merely keeps it intact.

FD is ideal for short-term objectives (such as saving for a vacation in 6 months or for a reserve fund).

But long-term wealth generation requires assets that appreciate at a rate higher than inflation.

Reflection Question: Do you wish for money to merely remain safe, or do you desire it to grow?

Various Kinds of Loans and Their Implications

Loans are not always evil. Some loans are instruments that assist you in building your future, while others lead to debt traps. The trick lies in knowing which is which.

Here's a simplified chart:

Type of Loan	Purpose / When Used	Approx. Interest Rate (India, 2025)	Good / Risky?
Home Loan	Buying a house/property	8% – 9% p.a.	Good (asset creation, tax benefits)

Education Loan	Funding higher studies	9% – 11% p.a.	Good (if course improves earning power)
Auto Loan	Buying a car/bike	9% – 11% p.a.	Risky (asset depreciates)
Gold Loan	Quick cash against gold	8% – 12% p.a.	Short-term only
Personal Loan	Medical, travel, wedding, and emergency expenses	11% – 18% p.a.	Risky (high interest, no asset created)
Credit Card Loan	Outstanding dues converted into EMIs	24% – 36% p.a.	Very Risky (avoid if possible)

Business Loan	Starting/expanding a business	9% – 15% p.a.	Good (if business generates higher returns)

Golden Rule: Borrow only to fund needs that generate value (home, education, business). Do not borrow to fund wants (gadgets, holidays, lifestyle).

What is a Mutual Fund?

Let's say you and nine friends have ₹1,000 each. Individually, you would be able to invest in very few shares of a business. But collectively, you have ₹10,000, a kitty large enough to invest in several businesses, bonds, and segments.

That's precisely what a Mutual Fund (MF) does.

The mutual fund is a collection of money held by many investors and put into a series of securities, stocks, bonds, or other securities. This is carried out under the supervision of seasoned fund managers who decide on where to invest as well as what to invest.

So, rather than you getting familiar with 50 companies, you just invest in a fund that has a diversified mix already.

Direct vs Indirect Funds (Regular):

Direct Mutual Fund: You invest directly from the Asset Management Company (AMC). Greater returns (no commission). You have to select and monitor funds on your own.

Regular/Indirect Mutual Fund: You invest through a distributor, broker, or advisor. Convenient for new investors (assistance offered). Lessor returns (distributor charges commission).

Rule of Thumb: If you're confident and willing to research, go for direct plans. If you're new and unsure, regular plans with guidance may help you start.

Different Types of Mutual Funds

Mutual funds are not "one size fits all." They come in different flavors, each serving a different purpose. Here's a breakdown:

Debt Funds

- Invest in bonds, government securities, and corporate debt.
- Lower risk, lower return (6–8%).
- Suitable for conservative investors or short-term goals.

Equity Funds

- Invest in the stocks of the company.
- High risk, high return (10–15% long run).
- Long-term wealth creation.

Types of Equity Funds

1. Large-Cap Funds: Invest in the top 100 large companies (stable, low risk).
2. Mid-Cap Funds: Invest in mid-sized companies (growth possibilities, moderate risk).
3. Small-Cap Funds: Invest in small companies (high growth, very high risk).
4. Multi-Cap Funds: A Combination of large, mid, and small caps (balanced diversification).

Index Funds

- Follow a market index (such as Nifty 50 or Sensex).
- Low-cost, passive management.
- Good for beginners looking for steady long-term growth.

Thematic Funds

- Invest in a particular theme (such as digital India, renewable energy, healthcare).

- Riskier because it rides on one theme performing well.

Sector Funds

- Invest in a single industry (IT, pharma, banking).
- It can give fabulous returns if the industry grows, but it can be risky if it crashes.

ELSS (Equity-Linked Savings Scheme)

- Tax-saving mutual fund under Section 80C of the Income Tax Act.
- 3-year lock-in (shortest for tax-saving options).
- Excellent choice for young professionals to save tax + accumulate wealth.

Here's a simple comparison chart for you to understand it better:

Type	Return Potential	Risk Level	Best For
Debt Fund	6–8%	Low	Short-term goals, safety

Large-Cap Fund	9–12%	Low–Medium	Beginners, stability
Mid-Cap Fund	12–15%	Medium–High	Long-term investors
Small-Cap Fund	15%+	High	Aggressive investors
Multi-Cap Fund	10–14%	Medium	Balanced portfolio
Index Fund	10–12%	Low–Medium	Beginners, passive investors
Thematic Fund	Varies	High	Risk-takers with conviction

Sector Fund	Varies	High	Focused bets
ELSS Fund	10–14%	Medium	Tax savers + long-term growth

The charm of mutual funds is diversification + professional handling. You don't have to research every company; you simply have to choose the right fund for your objective.

What is the Stock Market?

Look at the stock market as a gigantic bazaar, and there are no vegetables and clothes being sold. Instead, it is pieces of companies that are being handed over.

By buying the stock of a firm (also known as a share), you are buying a small portion of ownership in the given firm. If the firm does well and profits, your piece increases in value. If the firm does poorly, your piece loses value.

The stock market is merely the venue that facilitates this exchange.

There are two principal stock exchanges in India:

1. BSE (Bombay Stock Exchange) – one of Asia's oldest.
2. NSE (National Stock Exchange) – renowned for its contemporary, technology-based systems.

Stocks are listed on these exchanges via IPOs (Initial Public Offerings), enabling the public to purchase shares and become partial owners.

Why should this be important to you?

Because with the stock market, common folks (not billionaires alone) can invest in the growth of companies such as Infosys, HDFC, Reliance, or Zomato.

What is a Demat Account?

Years ago, stocks were paper pieces. You kept them physically, and if you lost them, you lost ownership. Nowadays, it's all digital.

A Demat Account (Dematerialised Account) is a virtual locker where all your shares are safely kept.

In order to invest in the stock market, you require two things:

Demat Account – keeps your shares in digital form.

Trading Account – allows you to buy/sell shares in the exchange.

Most brokers these days (such as Zerodha, Groww, Upstox, ICICI Direct, etc.) offer both combined into one app.

Visualize this:

Trading account = a store where you buy/sell.

Demat account = a locker in which you keep your purchases.

How to Begin Investing in Equities/Shares

Entering the stock market may intimidate you, but it's easier than ever:

Step 1: Open a Demat + Trading Account

1. Select a SEBI-registered broker (Zerodha, Groww, ICICI, HDFC Securities, etc.).
2. Do KYC (Aadhaar, PAN, Bank details).

Step 2: Fund Your Account

1. Transfer funds from your bank to your broker's wallet.

Step 3: Research Before You Buy

1. Begin with businesses you are familiar with and comprehend.
2. Examine their model, earnings, growth, and leverage.

Step 4: Begin Small

1. Don't immediately purchase hundreds of stocks. Start with 2-3 robust firms or, even safer, an Index Fund ETF (such as Nifty 50 ETF).

Step 5: Invest, Not Gamble

1. Steer clear of "hot tips" from Telegram channels or friends.
2. Don't buy/sell on a day-to-day market commotion.
3. Plan in terms of years, not days.

Golden Tips for Newbies

1. Begin with long-term investing, not day-to-day trading.
2. Invest money you do not need right now.
3. Diversify rather than betting the farm on a single stock.
4. You are not trying to be clever today. You are trying to make money steadily over decades.

Why Index Funds Are a Low-Risk Way for Beginners

Imagine this: rather than buying shares of a single company or a couple of companies that you do not know, you are buying shares of a set of companies. Hence, your risk is spread to many companies, while the return will be the average return of this set of companies.

That's what Index Funds do.

An Index Fund simply copies a market index (like the Nifty 50 or the Sensex).

If the index goes up, your fund goes up.

If it falls, your fund falls.

There's no active stock-picking; it just mirrors the market.

Why this is great for beginners:

- Low Risk: You're investing in 50 or 100 companies at once, not just one.
- Low Cost: Fund managers don't "actively" manage it, so fees are minimal.
- Steady Growth: Indian indices such as Nifty 50 have historically provided ~10–12% returns per annum over decades.
- Beginner Friendly: You don't need to learn every company. You simply wager on India's economy to expand.

If you have no clue where to begin, begin with an Index Fund or ETF (Exchange-Traded Fund). It's the easiest method to create wealth without overcomplicating things.

Difference Between Investing & Trading

Most newbies mix the two up. Let's settle this once and for all.

Investing:

- Long-term (years/decades).
- Emphasis on the fundamentals of the company (profits, growth, potential).
- Target = Wealth generation, inflation beating.
- Example: Investment in Infosys stock for holding it for 10 years.

Trading:

- Short-term (minutes, hours, days, weeks).
- Emphasis on charts, patterns, and timing of the market.
- Target = Fast profit from movements in prices.
- Example: Investment in Infosys in the morning, selling it in the evening to earn a minor profit.

The Trap: Many youngsters jump into trading thinking it's an easy way to make money.

In reality, 90% of traders lose money in the long run because emotions (fear/greed) overpower strategy.

Lesson: If you're a beginner, invest. Don't trade unless you've studied deeply and can afford to lose.

Importance of Diversification

You've probably heard the saying: "Don't put all your eggs in one basket."

In finance, this is referred to as diversification, splitting your money into various assets so that one bust will not ruin you.

Why diversification is important:

If you put all your money in one stock and it crashes, you are ruined.

If you split into 10–15 companies, even if 2–3 bust, the others counterbalance it.

Aside from stocks, you must also diversify into debt funds, gold, property, and even foreign funds.

Real Example:

In 2020, aviation shares plummeted because of COVID. Whoever invested everything in aviation lost a lot of money.

But whoever had diversified in IT, pharma, FMCG, and gold still got decent returns overall.

It is not about seeking maximum gain. It's about minimizing risk and sleeping soundly at night.

Reflection Question: Suppose tomorrow your primary investment fell by 30% in value. Would you remain financially sound, or would it ruin you?

Investing in Gold/Silver Without Actually Purchasing It

Indian families have relied on gold and silver as symbols of prosperity and security for generations. However, holding physical gold involves issues like problems, theft danger, storage fees, making fees, and even the urge to sell during emergencies.

Now, smarter options are available through technology:

Gold ETFs (Exchange-Traded Funds)

- Operates like a mutual fund but is gold-backed.
- Listed on the stock market.
- No making charges, no storage issue.
- Minimum investment = as low as 1 unit (≈ 1 gram of gold).
- Regulated by SEBI

Sovereign Gold Bonds (SGBs)

- Issued by the Government of India.

- Follows gold price movements + provide an additional 2.5% interest each year.
- Get held in Demat form.
- Lock-in: 8 years (but may withdraw after 5).
- Ideal for long-term investors seeking safety + returns.

Digital Gold

- Provided by apps such as Paytm, PhonePe, and Google Pay.
- You can invest as low as ₹10 in the value of gold.
- Secured by actual gold held in vaults by the provider.
- Flexible but ensure the platform is reliable.
- High risk since it is not regulated by authorities like SEBI or RBI

Silver ETFs / Funds

- Newer alternative in India, just like Gold ETFs.
- Allows you to invest in silver without having to worry about storage.

The plus of these financial/digital kinds of gold and silver is that they help keep money, are liquid to purchase/sell, and eliminate the hassles of physical storage.

Closing Story – Neha's Smart Shift

Neha, a 28-year-old marketing executive, grew up seeing her mother invest in gold jewelry and her father hold on to FDs. When Neha began working, she did the same: FDs for "security" and gold bangles for "investment."

But with time, she observed something peculiar.

As her jewelry collection increased, so did her spending. The FDs hardly kept up with the inflation rate.

Her friends, on the other hand, were investing in index funds and mutual funds, and their money was compounding.

One day, her younger co-worker described, "Gold isn't just jewelry anymore. You can invest in Sovereign Gold Bonds, safer, smarter, and tax-efficient."

That conversation transformed Neha's perspective.

She started to move:

- 30% of savings in index funds.
- 20% in SGBs.
- 40% in diversified equity/debt mutual funds.
- 10% retained liquid for contingencies.

After five years, Neha was not only "saving", she was growing.

She had outrun inflation, had no debt, and even convinced her parents to invest in SGBs rather than buying jewelry.

Neha's experience indicates that wealth is not created by blindly copying old ways.

It is created by learning, conforming, and diversifying intelligently.

Final Takeaway

This Bonus Chapter has been your crash course in the next level of financial literacy:

- Saving is earning, but only when you protect it from inflation.
- FDs are secure but not wealth generators.
- Loans can be a help or a hindrance, so choose carefully.
- Mutual funds and index funds are entry-level gateways to growth.
- Stock markets are mighty but need discipline and patience.
- Diversification is your armor.
- Gold and silver can shield wealth without having to occupy your locker.

Money isn't about fear or greed.

It's about clarity.

And once you understand these tools, you no longer feel at the mercy of inflation, banks, or market noise. You feel in control.

Just like Neha

www.ingramcontent.com/pod-product-compliance
Lightning Source LLC
Chambersburg PA
CBHW041302210926
51847CB00010B/108
* 9 7 8 9 3 9 1 3 1 7 8 0 5 *